WRITINGS TO YOUNG WOMEN ON

LAURA INGALLS WILDER

AS TOLD BY HER FAMILY, FRIENDS,
AND NEIGHBORS

VOLUME THREE

Laura Ingalls Wilder
Edited by Stephen W. Hines

Tommy nelson™
FOR TWEENS AND TEENS

A Division of Thomas Nelson Publishers
Since 1798

www.thomasnelson.com

Writings to Young Women on Laura Ingalls Wilder:
As Told by Her Family, Friends, and Neighbors
Volume Three
Adapted from *I Remember Laura*
Copyright © 2006 by Stephen W. Hines
Cover design by Lookout Design, Inc.

Published in Nashville, Tennessee, by Tommy Nelson®, a Division of Thomas Nelson, Inc. Visit us on the Web at www.tommynelson.com.

Tommy Nelson® books may be purchased in bulk for educational, business, fund-raising, or sales promotional use. For information, please e-mail:
SpecialMarkets@ThomasNelson.com.

Scripture quotations are taken from *The Holy Bible, King James Version*.

This book is not in any way sponsored by or affiliated with HarperCollins Publishers, which claims the exclusive right to use the words "Little House" as a trademark. Our use of these words simply and truthfully brings to you the warm personal facts about Laura Ingalls Wilder, America's beloved author, and about her life, times, and beliefs.

Cover photograph credits: Rose's graduation photo (Herbert Hoover Presidential Library), Almanzo on Rocky Ridge Farm (The Kansas State Historical Society), Cover of the *Missouri Ruralist* (The Kansas State Historical Society), Irene and James Lichty (courtesy of James Lichty), Laura and dolls (courtesy of Nava Austin), Laura signing books (courtesy of the *Springfield News-Leader*), Rose as baby (South Dakota State Historical Society), Rose on walking tour (Herbert Hoover Presidential Library), Laura and Rose at creek (South Dakota State Historical Society).

Library of Congress Cataloging-in-Publication Data

Wilder, Laura Ingalls, 1867-1957.
    [Prose works. Selections]
    Writings to young women from Laura Ingalls Wilder / Laura Ingalls Wilder ; edited by Stephen W. Hines.
        p. cm.
    ISBN 1-4003-0786-4 (*As Told by Her Family, Friends, and Neighbors*, Volume Three)
    1. Young women—Conduct of life. I. Hines, Stephen W. II. Title.
PS3545.I342A6 2006
814'.52—dc22

                                                                                2005033723

Printed in the United States of America

06 07 08 09 10 WRZ 9 8 7 6 5 4 3 2 1

CONTENTS

CONTENTS

FOREWORD

To hear people talk of Laura Ingalls Wilder, as I did, there was really nothing special to talk about, though she had become famous in the midst of a very small community. Mrs. Wilder, as she was generally called, had been a part of the life of Mansfield, Missouri, since 1894, and her first book hadn't been published until 1932.

By then, town folk and country folk alike were so used to her, they probably never thought of Mrs. Wilder as a writer, let alone one who received hundreds and sometimes thousands of fan letters from all over the world. Swamped by the flood of mail, Laura had to send out a form reply when the volume became too much.

However, that first impression I had of how her neighbors regarded Mrs. Wilder was soon replaced by other impressions. Behind the commonplace elements of her everyday life in Missouri, there was a woman of imagination and even eccentricity. Here was a practical farmer's wife, not the least bit sentimental about most animals, who set a place at the table for the family dog! Not only that, but the beloved pet was trained to carry messages attached to his collar to the "Man of the Place," so Almanzo would know when to come to lunch.

Also, the Wilders lived near a flowing stream, from which they used to haul water before they were able to have it piped in. No one knows quite how it happened, but eventually turtles from the creek flocked to Laura's back door to be fed. How she knew what turtles would eat is a mystery. Maybe they ate what the dog left behind.

I think most young people would have liked Mrs. Wilder if they could have known her, even in her old age. The young girl and the older woman weren't that different.

As you read through this book, you will find many different opinions expressed about whether the Wilders were outgoing, lonely, or reclusive. Many observers make for many different opinions, and Mrs. Wilder probably changed over the years as did those who knew her.

In 1957 Mrs. Wilder passed away, but the memory of her lingers on in her writings and in the hearts of the dwindling few who knew her personally.

Stephen W. Hines
Editor

ACKNOWLEDGMENTS

A book of this sort is made up of the work of many help-ing hands. I can only acknowledge a few of the dozens of people who have contributed toward making this book happen. I especially thank my wife for her patience during this project.

For their interviews or for general help in pointing me toward places where I could find information about Laura Ingalls Wilder, I wish to thank James A. Lichty, Iola Jones, Roscoe Jones, Sheldon Jones, Neta Seal, Nava Austin, Larry Dennis, Erman and Peggy Dennis, Sondra Gray, Madge Matlock, Suzanne Lippard, Mrs. M. J. Huffman, Mrs. Tom Carter, Don Brazeal, Imogene Green, Darrell Hunter, the Reverend and Mrs. Carleton Knight, Alvie Turner, Tom Carnall, Mrs. Floyd Cooley, Debbie Von Behren, Alvin Goldberg, Dorothy A. Buenemann, W. D. Le Count, Arlen Le Count, Paul and Arlene Magnin, Francis G. Thayer, Donald Harding, Emogene Fuge, Aleene Kindel, Mrs. Florence Vanderneut, Lois Morris, Betty Haskell, Addie

Paradise, Professor Elliott Hollister, and Professor Ann Thomas Moore.

I wish to also thank L. Z. Drummond, my brother-in-law, for his research work. These people were also vital to my research: Dwight M. Miller, Senior Archivist, Herbert Hoover Presidential Library; Jim E. Detlefsen, audio-visual department, Herbert Hoover Presidential Library; Connie Dowcett, copyright administrator, the *Christian Science Monitor*; Clyde A. Rowan, President of the Wright County Historical and Genealogical Society; Dr. Leon Raney, Dean of Libraries, South Dakota State University; Laura Glum, Archivist, South Dakota State Archives; LaVera Rose, Manuscript Curator, South Dakota Historical Society; Fae Sotham, Editorial Secretary, The State Historical Society of Missouri; Nancy Sherbert, Curator of Photographs, Kansas State Historical Society; and Darrell Garwood, audio-visual collection, Kansas State Historical Society.

I wish to thank photographers Franklin Robertson and Arlene Magnin for the use of their individual photos.

For their editorial skills I wish to thank Janet Thoma, Susan Salmon Trotman, Laurie Clark, and Brian Hampton who were all once with Janet Thoma Books.

Also my thanks to Michael S. Hyatt, my former agent.

And special thanks to Jennifer Gingerich, Backlist Editor for Tommy Nelson, for making this current project possible.

ONE

"LITTLE TOWN ON THE PRAIRIE"—DE SMET, SOUTH DAKOTA

*"Only one pioneer prairie town has
ever sprung to life, out of almost nothing,
to establish itself on the wide prairie."*

Introduction to the De Smet Era

Although there are tens of thousands of small western towns dotting this country—all of them with a pioneer past and cast of characters—only one town really stands out with any distinctiveness in American literature: De Smet, South Dakota. For Laura Ingalls Wilder readers, officially numbered in the tens of millions by now, only one pioneer prairie town has ever sprung to life, out of almost nothing, to establish itself on the wide prairie. That town is De Smet, South Dakota, of course, the "Little Town on the Prairie." De Smet and its environs are the setting for five of Mrs. Wilder's classic books.

Yet such is the power of television that if you surveyed the vast body of American TV viewers, they might well name that town as Walnut Grove, Minnesota. That's where the late Michael Landon and cast held sway with viewers for over ten years. For them Walnut Grove was the arche-typal prairie town our forefathers settled. That's TV for you.

A remembrance of Mrs. Wilder must begin in De Smet, South Dakota, the place that forged Laura's personality. A brief list of the events that occurred in De Smet show you their importance to both Laura and to her stories:

Early in 1879	Pa Ingalls moves to Dakota Territory to work for the Chicago & Northwestern Railroad.
September 1879	The Ingalls family settles near Silver Lake.
Later in 1879	The Ingallses move into a surveyors' house for the winter.
Spring 1880	The family moves to their homestead claim south of De Smet.
October 1880	The Ingallses move into Pa's store in town after the first blizzard of what is to be the Long Winter.
November 1881	Mary leaves for the Iowa School for the Blind in Vinton, Iowa.
December 1882	Laura receives her teacher's certificate and teaches at Brewster school. Although a short term, it is a miserable experience.

1884	Almanzo Wilder proposes to Laura, who is seventeen.
August 25, 1885	Laura and Almanzo marry at the Reverend Edward Brown's home, without any members of Laura's family being present.
December 5, 1886	The couple's daughter, Rose, is born.
Summer 1888	Laura and Almanzo's baby boy, who is never named, dies after living two weeks. They have no more children.
August 1889	Laura and Almanzo's house burns. Laura blames herself.

In May of 1890 Laura and Almanzo moved to Spring Valley, Minnesota, with Almanzo's folks. They lived there—except for a brief sojourn in Florida—for four years until September of 1894, when they moved to Mansfield, Missouri, the town in which they spent the rest of their lives.

Laura lived in De Smet, South Dakota, for eleven years, a long time for the wandering Ingalls family. I begin the De Smet part of this book with a poem Laura wrote in 1930, when she was unable to attend the Old Settlers' Day celebration that marked the fiftieth anniversary of the founding of the town.

Let's begin by letting Laura tell us, in her own words, what the Dakota prairies meant to her.

—Stephen W. Hines

The surveyors' house just as it was when the Ingallses lived there in 1879.

Dakota Prairies
A Poem by Laura Ingalls Wilder

Nobody knows when Laura first began writing poetry, but it was her habit from an early age to put down her feelings in verse. An unpublished collection of Laura's poetry shows that the youthful poet had a good sense of humor, strong opinions, and a sensitive eye for landscape. Although the beauties of nature are frequently extolled in her verse, she was quite versatile and in later years composed a song for her beloved Mansfield Athenian Club.

The fact is, poetry for common people was much more in vogue during Laura's early years than it is today. Practically every newspaper from great to small published verse, and there were numerous women's magazines to which one might contribute.

Laura was already well established as a journalist when she penned the following for the De Smet town celebration of Old Settlers' Day.

DAKOTA PRAIRIES

Ever I see them in my mental vision
As first my eyes beheld them years agone;
Clad all in brown with russet shades and golden
Stretching away into the far unknown;
Never a break to mar their sweep of grandeur,
From North to South, from East to West the same,
Save that the East was full of purple shadows,
The West with setting sun was all aflame;
Never a sign of human habitation
To show that man's domain was begun;
The only marks the footpaths of the bison
Made by the herds before their day was done.
The sky down-turned a brazen bowl to me,
And clanging with the calls of wild gray geese
Winging their way unto the distant Southland
To 'scape the coming storms and rest in peace.
Ever the winds went whispering o'er the prairies,

Ever the grasses whispered back again,
And then the sun dipped down below the skyline,
And stars lit just the outline of the plain.

Child of the Prairie
The Personal Recollections of Neva Whaley Harding

"Child of the Prairie," Neva Harding (née Whaley) was one of the early pioneers of South Dakota. She and her family arrived in the town of De Smet, South Dakota, in the summer that preceded the famous "Hard Winter" of 1880–81.

That was a summer full of hope. The new community was filling fast with settlers who had already been driven from hearth and home by failures elsewhere. Some had left in the middle of the night to avoid creditors. Some had seen little children die on the way. These folks hoped that Dakota Territory would be their stopping place, the bustling beginnings of De Smet a good omen of their own fresh start as well.

The Ingalls family—Charles and Caroline and their daughters Mary, Laura, Carrie, and Grace—important members of the De Smet community, were already settled in a claim shanty just southeast of town. Mutual friends of the Whaley and Ingalls families were the Boasts, Rob and Ella, who had spent the previous winter in a shanty very near the Ingalls. These stalwart people seemed to offer promise that

8

what was sprouting from the plain was not a mirage but a sturdy community.

Carrie Ingalls became one of Neva Whaley's best friends when they met at the first De Smet school. Their teacher, V. S. L. Owen, had come to teach after the rather unsuccessful tenure of "lazy, lousy 'Liza Jane" Wilder, Almanzo's older, "bossy" sister. Miss Wilder, a pioneer homesteader in her own right, was Laura Ingalls's nemesis for the duration of their teacher/pupil relationship. Later, Laura came to trust Eliza Jane so much that she sent her daughter, Rose, to live with Eliza Jane so Rose could continue her education at a quality high school in Louisiana.

The following memoir by Neva Whaley Harding, "I Recall Pioneer Days in South Dakota," is a collage of memories of early De Smet, prominently featuring the Ingallses and the Boasts.

I RECALL PIONEER DAYS IN SOUTH DAKOTA

My father, Josiah Whaley, came to Dakota in the spring of 1880, leaving Mother, my four-year-old brother, and me, eight years old, to stay near an uncle in Mantorville, Minnesota. Dad stopped off at various towns along the Chicago & Northwestern Railroad but went on to Huron, the end of the line. Huron gave promise of being a good business town, and Dad felt it would be a good place to locate. But sometimes very small things decide the path of one's life. The water at Huron made him quite ill, so he decided to settle at De Smet where, he recalled, the water was fine.

Even at that early date, claims around De Smet had all been filed on, but for a small sum Dad was able to buy a relinquishment on a quarter section three miles east of town.

As the Vermillion River flowed southward, it overflowed into Silver Lake at flood time. On the south bank of the lake, a little south and east of De Smet, lived the Ingalls family. The Boasts told us a lot about the Ingalls family, having lived with them the winter of 1879–80. I did not meet Laura until later when I attended the De Smet school. (Had I known how famous she was to become, I might have struggled through the tall slough grass among muskrat houses and cattails to her door; might even, perchance, have met her the time she tells of getting lost in that same slough.)

> Had I known how famous she was to become, I might have struggled through the tall slough grass among muskrat houses and cattails to her door.

Dad, who liked to work with wood, had owned a sawmill back in Pennsylvania; but, there being no wood to saw in Dakota, he took to building houses. Besides working in De Smet that first summer, he managed to enclose a house for us on the claim and planned to finish it on the inside during the winter. It was rather a good house for those days—two fair-sized rooms and two small ones, several degrees better than a claim shanty. Nearly all houses could be built from lumber shipped in; there was only one sod house in our neighborhood.

LAURA INGALLS WILDER

Laura Ingalls was born in Wisconsin, 1867. . . . To seek a new home, the family set out in a covered wagon, living for a time in Missouri, Indian Territory, Kansas, Nebraska, Minnesota, and finally settling on a claim near De Smet, Dakota Territory, on the shore of Silver Lake in 1877 or 1878 [1879]. Mr. Ingalls traveled with his wife and four daughters: Laura, then about ten years old; Mary, who was blind; and Carrie and Grace. (I advise tourists not to seek out Silver Lake. Better keep your sentimental picture of it as given by Laura. It was first thought to be a likely place for a slaughter house and for years was used as a city dump; now it is nearly filled up.)

> There was such sparkle and life in her expression that she was very attractive.

The family spent summers on the claim and winters in town. I think Mr. Ingalls was timekeeper for the C&NW Railroad, then under construction. I knew the family quite

well, especially Carrie. Laura was about sixteen and fin-
ishing her last year of school when I arrived. Schools were
not graded then, but she was in about the eighth grade.
She was fortunate in having for a teacher Professor V. S. L.
Owen, who gave pupils thorough instruction in the basic
subjects. He recognized Laura's talent for writing and
advised her to keep on with it, but she did not do so until
she was about sixty-five years old. As a girl Laura was a
medium blond with large blue eyes. She could hardly
have been called pretty, but there was such sparkle and
life in her expression that she was very attractive.

After leaving school she taught for a short time and
then married a neighbor farmer boy, Almanzo Wilder,
known as "Manly." They lived for awhile near De Smet
where their daughter, Rose, was born in 1887 [1886].
Mr. Wilder was very fond of horses and always drove a
"spanking" team.

Laura and her husband soon developed wanderlust. I
expect that if they had lived today, they would have
bought a trailer. As it was, they followed in her father's
footsteps and fitted out a covered wagon and set out to
see the world. They tarried for a time in several states. In
1894, they finally came to rest at Mansfield, Missouri, in
the northern part of the beautiful Ozarks, where they
lived the rest of their lives on a little farm. This is where
she wrote her eight books, all about her own family
home life in the various places they had lived.

Almanzo Wilder, whom Laura often referred to as
"The Man of the Place"

All the people she mentions are real people with their real names. Her first book was published in 1932 when she was sixty-five. These books are referred to as children's classics; no library is complete without them.

Laura took an active interest in community life and often wrote articles for farm papers. She outlived the rest of her family and died at the age of ninety. She had been a serene, contented, home-loving woman with a keen interest in the world as it passed by her door.

TWO

CELEBRATED AUTHOR: THE MANSFIELD ERA

"We believe her books will live and will be read with interest a hundred years from now just as they are today."

Introduction to the Mansfield Era

Laura's fame has always bewildered her adopted town of Mansfield. She lived as a farmer's wife and an active rural neighbor to the town for almost forty years before writing a published book under the name Laura Ingalls Wilder.

By the time she did this radical thing of writing a book, her daughter, Rose, was the town's famous cosmopolitan citizen, a world traveler who had eschewed travel to return to her native village—population approximately eight hundred—to write. The town recognized Mrs. Wilder as a former correspondent for the *Missouri Ruralist*. But by her late fifties she had given up even that modest task, and the Wilders were supposedly in retirement. Thus, it took Mansfield many years to become reconciled to Mrs. Wilder's latter-day fame as a famous storyteller. Indeed, most people you talk to will begin with an apology: "If I had only known that she would become famous, I would have paid more attention to what she said and did."

Certainly people in Mansfield had little idea of the importance of her books, as you can see from the following artless, but appreciative book review of *Little House on the Prairie*, which appeared in her local paper on October 3, 1935. Surely it must have delighted as well as amused Mrs. Wilder:

Mrs. Laura Ingalls Wilder have our thanks for a copy of her very latest book, "The Little House on the Prairie." The book has been read, every word, and a very interesting book it is.

It goes back to her childhood life of pioneer days when she left the "Little House in the Woods," in Wisconsin, with her parents, in a covered wagon and came to the Kansas plains where they built their little house and started life anew, only to last a year at that place.

From the very beginning of the book, every paragraph is so absorbing till one loses sight of the present time and

> "A good friend to books is a good friend to have."

drifts back to the plain and meager way of living and all of which was happy. One pictures in their mind each character which were Pa and Ma, Mary, Laura, and baby Carrie. Their constant and ever faithful watchdog and their good mustang ponies, Pet and Patty.

Every chapter has a thrill. How they built their little house, the children playing 'round the door, the chimney catching on fire when Pa was away one windy day, the wolves howling, Indians on a war dance that lasted for a week, and a number of other exciting things.

The book holds the interest of the reader till one becomes in mind. A character of it. Living simple and happy in God's great universe. We read this book evenings. Retire and our minds run on, of the real experiences of this happy little family of many years ago.

Mrs. Wilder's book, "Farmer Boy," which was published more than a year ago, was adopted as a textbook in many schools. We have not read this book but understand it is one of the most interesting. We are indeed very proud of the book. You know some writer one time said, "A good friend to books is a good friend to have."

This ending quote, "A good friend to books is a good friend to have," sums up Mansfield's impression of Laura Ingalls Wilder.

The people of Mansfield, Missouri, claimed Laura as their own. And they claimed some credit for influencing her life. Debbie Von Behren, award-winning teacher, native of the town, and freelance writer, summarized this feeling in *Mansfield: First One Hundred Years*:

> We aren't the only town in America to claim Laura Ingalls Wilder for our own. Every community she has lived in wants some of the glory of having had a famous citizen. Well, I hate to disappoint them, but I think Laura especially belongs to Mansfield. She and Almanzo chose our town, she lived here for over 60 years, and most important, she wrote every single one of her books here.
>
> We know Laura was special. But there also has to be something special about the town that provided the environment necessary for her talent to shine through.

Certainly Mansfield has its place in any reminiscence of Laura Ingalls Wilder. A quick look at the events that occurred during the sixty years Laura lived here show how important this era of her life was to her writing career:

1894	Laura and Almanzo purchase Rocky Ridge Farm.
1911	Laura starts to write for the *Missouri Ruralist*.
1932	Laura's first book, *Little House in the Big Woods*, is published.
1933	*Farmer Boy* is published.
1935	*Little House on the Prairie* is published.

1937	*On the Banks of Plum Creek* is published.
1940	*The Long Winter* is published.
1943	*Little Town on the Prairie* and *These Happy Golden Years* are published. (Wilder's books are available from HarperCollins Publishers.)
1947	Garth Williams, illustrator of such books as *Stuart Little*, retraces the Ingallses' journey as he works on illustrating a new edition of the books.
October 23, 1949	Almanzo Wilder dies at the age of 92 and is buried in Mansfield.
February 10, 1957	Laura Ingalls Wilder dies at the age of 90 and is buried in Mansfield.

The Mansfield years tell us a great deal about who Laura was and how she lived. Let's begin these Mansfield years now with an article that introduced readers to Laura as one of the columnists of the *Missouri Ruralist*: "Let's Visit Mrs. Wilder."

Let's Visit Mrs. Wilder
Interview in the *Missouri Ruralist*
FEBRUARY 20, 1918

By John F. Case

Laura Ingalls Wilder had written regularly for the Missouri Ruralist *since 1916. Mr. John Case, editor of the* Ruralist, saw Mrs. Wilder's talent and unique observations and wanted to further her career—and the influence of the Ruralist among women. Mr. Case can truly be said to be the first significant journalist to recognize Laura's talent. He also noted that by the age of fifty she had already led a full life. Yet it would be fifteen more years before her first book would be published to wide acclaim! Mr. Case had no idea what he was starting.

"I was born in a log house within four miles of the legend-haunted Lake Pepin in Wisconsin," Mrs. Wilder wrote when I asked for information about her. "I remember seeing deer that Father had killed hanging in the trees about our forest home. When I was four years old, we traveled to the Indian Territory—Fort Scott, Kansas, being our nearest town. My childish memories hold the sound of the war whoop, and I see pictures of painted Indians."

> "My childish memories hold the sound of the war whoop, and I see pictures of painted Indians."

Looking at the picture of Mrs. Wilder, which was recently taken, we find it difficult to believe that she is old enough to be the pioneer described. But having confided her age to the editor (not for publication), we must be convinced that it is true. Surely Mrs. Wilder, who is the mother of Rose Wilder Lane, talented author and writer, has found the fountain of youth in the Ozark hills. We may well believe that she has a "cheerful disposition" as her friend asserts.

"I was a regular little tomboy," Mrs. Wilder confesses, "and it was fun to walk the two miles to school." The folks were living in Minnesota then, but it was not long until Father Ingalls, who seems to have had a penchant for moving about, had located in Dakota. It was at De Smet, South Dakota, that Laura Ingalls, then eighteen years old, married A. J. Wilder, a farmer boy. "Our daughter, Rose Wilder Lane, was born on the farm," Mrs. Wilder informs us, "and it was there I learned to do all kinds of farm work with machinery. I have ridden the binder, driving six horses. And I could ride. I do not wish to appear conceited, but I broke my own ponies to ride. Of course, they were not bad, but they were broncos." Mrs. Wilder had the spirit that brought success to the pioneers.

> "I was a regular little tomboy," Mrs. Wilder confesses, "and it was fun to walk the two miles to school."

Mr. Wilder's health failed and the Wilders went to Florida. "I was something of a curiosity, being the only 'Yankee girl' the inhabitants ever had seen," Mrs. Wilder relates. The low altitude did not agree with Mrs. Wilder, though, and she became ill. It was then that they came

Courtesy of Nava Austin

Laura in her late sixties

to Rocky Ridge Farm near Mansfield, Wright County [Missouri], and there they have lived for twenty-five years. Only forty acres were purchased, and the land was all timber except a four-acre, worn-out field. "Illness and traveling expenses had taken our surplus cash, and we lacked $150 of paying for the forty acres," Mrs. Wilder writes. "Mr. Wilder was unable to do a full day's work. The garden, my hens, and the wood I helped saw and which we sold in town took us through the first year. It was then I became an expert at the end of a cross-cut saw, and I still can 'make a hand' in an emergency. Mr. Wilder says he would rather have me help than any man he ever sawed with. And, believe me, I learned how to take care of hens and to make them lay."

> I love to work. And it is a pleasure to write. And, oh, I do just love to play!

One may wonder that so busy a person, as Mrs. Wilder has proved to be, can find time to write. "I always have been a busy person," she says, "doing my own housework, helping the Man of the Place when help could not be obtained; but I love to work. And it is a pleasure to write. And, oh, I do just love to play! The days never have been long enough to do the things I would like to do. Every year has held more of interest than the year before." Folks who possess that kind of spirit get a lot of joy out of life as they travel the long road.

JOINED THE FAMILY IN 1911

Mrs. Wilder has held numerous important offices, and her stories about farm life and farm folks have appeared in the best farm papers. Her first article printed [for us] appeared in February 1911. It was a copy of an address prepared for *Farmer's Week*. So for seven years she has been talking to Missouri women through these columns, talk that always has carried inspiration and incentive for worthwhile work.

Reading Mrs. Wilder's contributions, most folks doubtless have decided that she is a college graduate. But "my education has been what a girl would get on the frontier," she informs us. "I never graduated from anything and only attended high school two terms."

Folks who know Mrs. Wilder, though, know that she is a cultured, well-educated gentlewoman. Combined with inherent ability, unceasing study of books has provided the necessary education, and greater things have been learned from the study of life itself.

The Life of Laura Ingalls Wilder
Feature Article in the *Mansfield Mirror*
SEPTEMBER 18, 1986

On February 7, 1867, a little girl was born to Charles and Caroline Ingalls. The baby was christened Laura

Elizabeth. She was the second daughter of four to be born to the Ingallses.

The daughter to precede Laura in birth was Mary Amelia (January 10, 1865). With these two daughters and wife, Charles Ingalls farmed a small farm in Wisconsin that was later to be known as "Little House in the Big Woods."

But Pa Ingalls was a pioneer and could not stand to stay in one place for long at one time, so he bundled up his three ladies and put them into a covered wagon and headed for Montgomery County, Kansas. Here in the family's second log cabin, Charles started farming anew.

A wonderful event came to grace the Ingallses again when their third daughter Carrie was born on August 3, 1870. But their life there was to be short-lived, for the government decided that the settlers were on Indian land and must either move out or be moved out by federal troops. Charles packed up his family once again and moved on to Minnesota.

In Plum Creek, Minnesota, the family seemed at last to have found a home where

> In Plum Creek, Minnesota the family seemed at last to have found a home where they could stay and prosper.

they could stay and prosper. There was a school for the girls to attend and a church to join, and it appeared to be Jordan across from Canaan. Even a son, Charles Frederick, was born to the Ingallses on November 1, 1875 [he died in 1876]. But the good times were not to continue, for grasshoppers ruined the Ingallses' crops and work was then very hard to find for Pa Ingalls. He was forced to travel far and wide to find the funds to feed his growing family.

So it was decided to move again. The family of six now (Grace Pearl, May 23, 1871 [1877]) headed for Burr Oak, Iowa. They stayed for only a short time and then returned to Minnesota.

Trouble plagued the family in 1879 when all the girls except Laura came down with scarlet fever. All survived, but Mary lost her sight for the rest of her life. The house was saddened by this unfortunate event, but a situation presented itself to Pa to take a job in De Smet in the Dakota Territory.

Pa worked for the railroad there and the family was very happy. Pa was able to homestead a claim and the girls were able to go to school and the family attended a church that they helped found, the De Smet First Congregational Church. Things were working out so well that even Mary, though blind, could still go to college.

Happiness was also in store for eighteen-year-old Laura. In 1885 she married Almanzo Wilder. Almanzo had a claim on some land near De Smet, and Laura helped him work it. In 1886 Almanzo and Laura Wilder presented their parents with a granddaughter named Rose.

Everything looked prosperous and full of happiness

and fullness of life for the Wilders in the Dakota Territory, but it was not to be. All of the crops were destroyed year after year by either hail or wind or drought or grasshoppers. Diphtheria struck the young family and almost destroyed Almanzo's health.

Fire took their home completely in 1889 and then came five years of drought from 1881 through 1885. They held on in the Dakota Territory until 1890 when they moved to Spring Lake, Minnesota.

After only a short time they decided that for Almanzo's sake they had better move to a better climate, so off they went to Florida. Florida did not suit the Wilders, and as Laura was to say to Irene Lichty, curator of the Wilder Home and Museum, many years later, "I will never go back to Florida as it is too low for me there."

By the middle of the year 1892, the family of three was back in De Smet where Almanzo did odd jobs to support his family. Laura assisted in the family finances by becoming a seamstress for a dollar a day. Rose, now age five, was allowed to attend school because her mother and father worked all day.

> She had been raised all of her life as a pioneer girl, and even when she married, she happened to pick another pioneer who loved to roam our beautiful country.

Laura Ingalls Wilder, though, had an ingrained sense of the pioneer. She had been raised all of her life as a pioneer girl, and even when she married, she happened to pick another pioneer who loved to roam our beautiful country. Almanzo decided that it was time to leave on yet another journey, and so, on July 17, 1894, the little family of three left for the Ozarks of Missouri.

The Wilders entered the state of Missouri on August 22, 1894. They arrived at what was to be their final home, Mansfield, after traveling 650 miles in 45 days. The Ozarks with its fall foliage in great array was no doubt a beautiful sight to three weary travelers who had been used to a dusty, windy, and hot climate like De Smet.

> Laura named their ground Rocky Ridge Farm.

With the hundred hard-earned dollars that Laura had saved from her long hours as a seamstress, she and Almanzo decided to buy a forty-acre plot of rocky, hilly land that was located one mile to the east of Mansfield. The hundred dollars went for the down payment. The entire plot of forty acres consisted of only five acres of cleared land, 400 unplanted apple trees, and a one-room windowless log cabin. Laura named their ground Rocky Ridge Farm.

The hard work of turning Rocky Ridge into a farm was just beginning and would take the Wilders many years to complete. Their neighbors pitched in, as all pioneer neighbors did, and helped Almanzo, Laura, and Rose build a hen house and a stable. Their first crop of corn was planted in 1895 along with potatoes. With egg and potato money, and money earned from the sale of wood and berries picked by Rose, the Wilders were finally able to purchase a pig and a cow.

A short time after their final home was started, the Wilders moved into Mansfield to make more money by taking in boarders and feeding the railroad workers that then resided in Mansfield. The house in which they lived in Mansfield was presented to the Wilders as a gift by Almanzo's father when he and his family came to visit in 1897. Just a few years later the Wilders decided that the farm was the place for them and they sold the Mansfield house and moved back to the farm just outside of Mansfield.

It was now decided that Rose would have to go elsewhere for her schooling, for she had about run to the limit of the amount of learning that could be obtained in Mansfield. Almanzo and Laura sent Rose to Louisiana to attend high school and live with Almanzo's sister, Eliza Jane. Rose was a good student, as always, and graduated in 1903.

Back at home at Rocky Ridge things were going very well. The farm in time would be up to 200 acres and the fruit from the farm would be making it all the way to markets in the big cities. Almanzo even brought in the Magnificent Morgan breed of horses to increase the quality of his own horses and that of his neighbors. Even the home was continuing to grow in size, taking better shape year by year. Almanzo spared no labor on the home that was going to be for his beloved Laura.

Laura's kitchen was considered to be, at one time, the most modern in the Ozarks. The home was finally completed in 1912 and was indeed an Ozark showplace.

More vistas that were not even dreamed about were to open for the now very content Almanzo and Laura. Laura had been making speeches concerning the raising of poultry which she did so well, and as she was unable to attend one of the meetings, she wrote out her speech so that it could be read. An editor of the *Missouri Ruralist* was in the audience and he offered Laura the job as home editor. She accepted.

> In February of 1911 Laura Ingalls Wilder was a writer!

In February of 1911, Laura Ingalls Wilder was a writer! Her writings about the raising of poultry and other farm tasks gradually gained access to many other newspapers and magazines. This added occupation also allowed Laura little extras for the home that she would not have otherwise had and also allowed her to travel to see her mother and sisters in De Smet. She even traveled to the west coast to visit Rose and her husband.

Back in Mansfield, Laura and Almanzo continued to work hard and prosper. Laura loved to work and to this end she took it upon herself to start a library at the county seat in Hartville and neighboring towns. She also became a member of many clubs and organizations, helping them to prosper with her hard work and dogged determination. Laura worked also with many women's farm clubs. Along this line, she worked with the Mansfield Farm Loan Association. She handed out almost a million dollars and not once was the money not repaid.

Rose Wilder Lane, Almanzo and Laura's daughter, was now becoming famous in her own right. Rose had been sent as a reporter to cover the war overseas. From her comments and articles the Wilders could follow her progress through many foreign lands. Rose was also writing books, two of which were *Henry Ford's Own Story* and *Peaks of Shala*. Rose came home to Rocky Ridge Farm after the war a wealthy person. She had a home built on the family land not far from the main house and lived there for several years.

Retirement was coming for the Wilders and when the new Highway 60 came through Rocky Ridge, the Wilders started selling off the land that had been their livelihood for 35 years. Many years Almanzo and Laura had worked for the day when they could sit back and rest and enjoy their well-deserved retirement.

The 1930s rolled in and Rose requested that Laura write down some of the old family stories so that they would not be lost. Laura complied and sent them to Rose thinking that Rose would write them into a book. Rose returned them to Laura and said, you write the book! So in 1932 at the age of 65, "retired" Laura Ingalls Wilder sent a book to Harper and Brothers entitled *Little House in the Big Woods*. A new career was just starting.

Mansfield Woman's Books Favored Both
by Children and Grown-ups
World Acclaim Has Come to Laura Ingalls Wilder
Whose Writings Cover Pioneer Life
Feature Article in the *Mansfield Mirror*

MAY 5, 1949

Mansfield, Mo., April 9—Stories of Middle Western American pioneer life which were written here on a school tablet with a pencil are being read around the world and by millions of Americans. Their author, Laura Ingalls Wilder, 82, is known and loved by countless school children. Their parents also like her "Laura and Mary" stories.

By all standards Mrs. Wilder is a famous American

author. Nevertheless, she is unaffected and as unassuming as in her earlier days when she helped "pull a crosscut saw" on Ozark timber.

This month the city of Detroit is paying high tribute to Mrs. Wilder. It is naming one of its new branch libraries for her. Other such libraries there bear some of the most famous names in American history.

Mrs. Wilder is the author of eight books that tell a story of everyday life in early Western America, extending from Wisconsin to the Dakotas and including adventures into the Indian territory of Kansas. Seven of the volumes are "Laura and Mary" stories, these characters being representative of Mrs. Wilder and a sister named Mary. The other book in the series is the story of a year in the boyhood life of her husband, Almanzo Wilder, who is 92 and a native of New York.

LIVE IN DISTINCTIVE HOME

This Ozark town of a little more than 1,000 population is 250 miles southwest of Kansas City. [Editor's note: This misstatement couldn't go by; "250 miles southwest of Kansas City" will put you in Oklahoma!] The Wilders live a half mile east of it. Their unpretentious, 2-story, white frame house sits on a hill overlooking U.S. Highway No. 60. It has a vine-covered stone chimney, tall and wide. Inside the home it is connected with a large fireplace in the living room—a room at once distinctive to a visitor because of its beamed ceiling and liberal use of woodwork, all white oak cut on the farm and shaped into lumber by the Wilders years ago. Except for the siding, most all materials used in building the home came right off the farm.

> "We worked hard, but it was interesting and didn't hurt us any."

The living room also has several wall cases and shelves for the many books of the family library and there are framed scrolls and other pieces of art, written or painted in tribute to Mrs. Wilder's stories.

Mr. and Mrs. Wilder have lived in this home on the land they call Rocky Ridge Farm since they moved here in a covered wagon from De Smet, S.D., in 1894. A drought lasting nearly three years had ruined most everything and everybody in the Dakotas, so the Wilders set out for the Ozarks, then known as "the land of the big red apples," seeking a new start in life.

They lived here in town for awhile, then acquired forty acres nearby, including a tree lien on the place. That proviso of the deal required that they carry out the terms of a former owner—to plant apple trees. The Wilders did, some ten acres at first, and their orchards were tended well enough that production reached proportions of carload shipments to Memphis, Tennessee, and other markets. Mrs. Wilder recalls that spraying was virtually unknown and unneeded in those days.

By the hardest of work in their earlier years here—Mrs. Wilder remembering well having helped to pull a saw on timber—they expanded their farm to more than 200 acres, had many chickens and dairy cattle, and kept farm work going until recent years.

"We worked hard, but it was interesting and didn't hurt us any," Mrs. Wilder says.

SHE RAISED CHICKENS

Their farm was made one of the most successful hereabouts. Mrs. Wilder raised the chickens and her husband handled the cows. Once they had a contest, she says, as to whether cows or chickens brought the biggest returns.

"We had to work against each other trying to prove our point," she adds with a brightening of the eyes, adding quickly that the contest "ended in a draw."

The Wilders take pride in their long years of work and in the success they made on their Ozark farmland. Mrs. Wilder is much less willing to talk of her success as a writer or of any claim to fame. She disdains having any display made over her writing, although it has attained a place that brings fan mail from Japan, Sweden, and other countries, as well as points all around America.

Her first writings were for newspapers and magazines, usually on poultry, or farming and rural subjects. It was not until 1932 that her first book was published and this event was more or less unexpected as far as she was concerned.

"Pa" Ingalls, her father, was a pioneer hunter, trapper, and Indian fighter. He guarded property of the Chicago-Northwestern railroad in the days it was being built, had many adventures in the Middle West and became one of the founders of De Smet, S.D.

Time after time she had heard him tell of his experiences, and her own part in the family activities are worth reading, as proven by book sales today.

> "I wrote between washing dishes and getting dinner, or just any time I could."

"These were family stories and I believed they should be preserved," Mrs. Wilder said, "so I wrote some of them down and sent them to my daughter Rose, so she could keep them. I also suggested she might want to use some of them in her writings."

Rose Wilder Lane, her daughter, who lives in Danbury, Connecticut, already was nationally known as a reporter and author.

"Rose wrote back, some time later," Mrs. Wilder continued, "that an editor had said the stories could be published if I would put some meat on the bones; so after that I started doing just that."

"I wrote between washing dishes and getting dinner,

or just any time I could," she added. "But sometimes I got stumped on a phrase or a chapter. Maybe the way to do it would not come to me until after I had gone to bed and then I would think of something in the middle of the night."

Thus the many duties of an active farm wife took on new chores, but highly worthwhile ones.

She used an ordinary pencil and school tablet. Her manuscripts were sent to New York for typing, and all business connected with the work of publication was and is handled by her agent. He is George T. Bye, former Kansas Citian, who handles the writing of Mrs. Franklin D. (Eleanor) Roosevelt, and other celebrities.

FAVORITE AMONG CHILDREN

Harper & Brothers of New York published the first book by Mrs. Wilder and all the others in the series. Chicago school children in 1947 selected Mrs. Wilder as their favorite author. She was honored in a special radio broadcast there. A plaque in the home here contains signatures of many Chicago children who took part in the events. Similar plaques have come from the Association of Children's Librarians of Northern California; also one from Seattle, representing children and librarians of the Pacific Northwest.

Her books are very popular with Kansas City Public Library patrons. "Pa's Fiddle," well known in the books now is in the state museum at Pierre, S.D., but is played every year in a special annual concert there.

With fame and extra cash from book royalties in recent years, most persons would say the golden years are certainly continuing, but writing success has its drawbacks these days, Mrs. Wilder finds.

HIT BY INCOME TAX

She doesn't talk in figures of the money she has received for her books, but she says: "The more I wrote the bigger my income tax got, so I stopped. Why should I go on at my age? Why, we don't need it here anyway."

The latter statement was in regard to her complete satisfaction with the simple, comfortable life in the home she has known for more than half a century, their home until the end of their days. But they still have a garden.

"I just finished planting the potatoes," said Mr. Wilder as he entered the home to greet visitors. Despite "not being strong" and his 92 years he is most alert to the current scene. Both the Wilders, however, complain of not being able to get help, "either inside or outside the house."

Detroit is planning appropriate ceremonies for the dedication of the library named for Mrs. Wilder. Officials there are eager for Mrs. Wilder to take part, but she says "definitely" she will not. It would be too much of a trip for Mr. Wilder, she adds; also, while she feels well, and certainly looks it, she says, "I'm too nervous" for anything like that.

Her last public appearance as an author was in Detroit six years ago when she took part in book week events there.

Ralph A. Ulveling, library director of Detroit, said recently that "we believe her books will live and will be read with interest a hundred years from now just as they are today. If our prediction is correct we will naturally take particular pride in having been the institution that led the way in bringing her permanent recognition among the American men and women of letters."

Others honored similarly by Detroit libraries include such famous Americans as Thomas Jefferson, Abraham Lincoln, and Thomas A. Edison, Ulveling noted. Seldom has the city so honored any living person.

"In choosing the name of Mrs. Wilder," Ulveling said, "we did so because we felt that she was a Midwestern writer who in her series of books has presented an invaluable social history of this great central portion of the country. While some historians, and they have an important place, present the great sweep of history, bringing out

> "We believe her books will live and will be read with interest a hundred years from now just as they are today."

the political and the military influences, Mrs. Wilder has directed attention to the commonplace things, the way of life of people. Thus she has preserved a portion of our history which is the part that is most likely to be lost in the course of time. She has done this beautifully, ably, and understandingly, and like so few writers she has done it in a way which is interesting both to children and to adults."

THREE

REMEMBERING LAURA

"She always had a list of little quotations
or sayings or poems that she kept in her head."

Friends and Travelers:
The Personal Recollections of Neta Seal

Neta Seal may be the genuine evidence that "they really don't make them like they used to." Devoted partner with her husband, Silas, she helped him build up his garage business in the small town of Mansfield, Missouri; owned rental property, which she continued to manage after his death; and took in washing for a time.

But Mrs. Seal was never too busy to be with people, and she is, at eighty-nine, just after a serious operation, still a people-person. One of the persons she grew attached to was Mrs. A. J. Wilder—Laura Ingalls Wilder.

Mrs. Seal first met Laura in the late thirties, and their friendship grew fast and strong throughout the remaining twenty years of Laura's life. Fortunately for us, Neta Seal has the remarkable attribute of a fine memory, and she has shared her knowledge of Mr. and Mrs. Wilder with hundreds of people over the years.

How we met the Wilders is sort of a long story. We came back from Detroit and bought a filling station, or a service station, we called it then, because it was all service.

One morning Almanzo came in and my husband checked his tires and cleaned his windshield and his windows and said, with a smile, "Mr. Wilder, what will you have?"

"Seal, you don't know whether I'm going to buy a dime's worth of gas from you," Mr. Wilder said, "but you give me all this free service, then ask me what I want."

"Well, Mr. Wilder, you need your windshield cleaned, and you need the right amount of air in your tires if you are going to drive," my husband replied. And that made a friend.

Mr. Wilder was always in there after that. He'd come into the service station and let Mrs. Wilder out—he called her Bessie and she called him Manly—to go to the grocery store, to the bank, or whatever she wanted to do. It was the kind of place where people gathered to talk. We sold gas and oil and all those things, and folks would just come down. I would say that Mrs. Wilder was the more outgoing and had a pretty good sense of humor.

By the time we got acquainted with them both, Mr. Wilder was crippled and used a cane. He walked with a limp and had one club foot. His shoe had to have a real thick sole, but I don't remember which foot it was. I think it was his right one, but I'm not sure.

Almanzo didn't have horses anymore; he had sold them. But he did have some goats. I can't remember exactly how many he had, maybe four or five, maybe six. He didn't have a big herd of them. These were milk goats, and he milked them by hand. He had a barn, and he had a little stand for them to step up on, and he'd go out there, and they'd come and jump up on it. He'd sit down and milk one; then he would turn that one out and let the next one in. But finally he got to where he couldn't take care of them so he sold them.

> I would say that Mrs. Wilder was the more outgoing and had a pretty good sense of humor.

They always had a dog up till old Ben died. He was a bulldog. They always had bulldogs after I got acquainted with them—I never knew them to have a cat.

Here's a funny little story about the dog. He had a boil on his jaw; and when it went to hurting him so bad, he'd come in and lay his head in her lap and look up as if he was saying, "Can you do anything for me?" Then she would get some salve and rub it on his jaw. When that was done, he would go back and lay down. Finally, it was healed.

Mrs. Wilder—I always called her Mrs. Wilder—didn't even have a dog after he went away [Almanzo died in 1949].

GOING WEST WITH THE WILDERS

You know, I did meet some of her family. We had come back from Detroit and had bought the filling station, but they were going to have to work on the streets, pave them or something. We didn't have anything to do, but Mr. Wilder wanted my husband to drive them on a trip to California [1938].

So my husband came in one day and asked me if I would like a trip to California with the Wilders. I hesitated a minute, then replied: "I don't know them well enough to make a long trip with them."

"Now is a good time to become acquainted. All it will cost us is money for our meals and lodging." You could get cabins for fifty cents a night then.

We left Mansfield early in May and got back by the end of the month.

SINGING WITH MRS. WILDER

On the trip we sang little crazy songs, Mrs. Wilder and I did, in the back seat, just to pass the time away:

Waltz me around old Willy,
Around and around and around.
And I'll give you some kisses
To make up for misses,
So waltz me around and around.

She loved that one because it was kind of fast. We'd just sing it over and over. Another one was "She Drives a Cadillac":

She drives a Cadillac;
I walk to work and back.
Oh boy, that's where my money goes.
My money goes
To buy my baby clothes.
(I buy her everything
for to keep her in style.)
She drives a little red Ford;
I ride the running board.
Oh boy, that's where my money goes.

While on our journey, Mr. Wilder was collecting branches to make walking canes. He really wanted a cane from each state in the Union. During a stop, he saw a tree he wanted a branch from for a cane. My husband cut the branch from the tree, and as they drove away, they came upon this sign: "This Park Protected by Law." They were certainly happy they hadn't been caught.

Mrs. Wilder tried to find a native Californian, but it seemed that everyone she talked to were natives of other states. One day we were sightseeing when Mrs. Wilder called excitedly, "I've found a native!" The man knew their daughter, Rose Wilder Lane, so they had a delightful visit with him.

Yes, it was quite a trip because we came back by way of the Black Hills of South Dakota. Laura's sister Carrie was living there in Keystone right by Mt. Rushmore. So we got us a cabin, and they stayed with Carrie.

> After that trip we were fast friends.

She was about the same size as Laura, small, and she was really nice. A year or two after this visit, Carrie came down to Mansfield to visit, and we were with them quite a while because we would take them driving to see different parts of the Ozarks.

Carrie's husband wasn't with her; he had died.

Laura's sister Grace was also still living over at De Smet. Grace was taller than either Laura or Carrie, as I remember. She was built more like Rose, but she was a little plump, not fat. I don't remember Grace visiting the Wilders in Mansfield while I knew them.

When we took that trip, I think Mrs. Wilder had finished

her books. Maybe not all of them. But she had done most of the writing. I got autographed copies of all of them. She gave me the full set with the statement: "You're not to loan these to anybody. If they want to read them they can go to the library or buy them. Because if you start loaning them out they'll be torn up, and they'll be lost and you won't have them." So I've never loaned them.

We weren't members of any of the same clubs, but after that trip we were fast friends. I was a Baptist and she was a Methodist, and I didn't attend a lot of clubs. They were both pretty much retired when we knew them. And they did have a modern farmhouse. Water was piped up to the house from a little ravine in back that had a spring. They also had indoor plumbing and a bathroom, though they didn't use modern heat. It was propane. We don't have natural gas down here even now.

THE FINAL YEARS

As I remember, Mrs. Wilder remained pretty healthy for a time even after Almanzo died. She did some sewing, crocheting, and embroidery, but not too much.

After he passed away, we went out there every Sunday afternoon to see her. We'd take her for drives. For a while she owned a Chrysler, I think, then she sold it.

There was a man by the name of Mr. Hartley here in town who was a taxi driver. So she finally let him go get her and bring her to town for the groceries. I had always done that and taken her to the bank, but I had this apartment house with four sleeping rooms I rented by night. It got to be too much work, so she let him drive her.

Helen Burkhiser did a book on me [Neta, Laura's Friend] that exhausted me when I saw what all I had done.

> Mrs. Wilder passed her time by doing a lot of reading, I think.

Mrs. Wilder passed her time by doing a lot of reading, I think. That was until her eyes failed. She did like to keep the radio on, but I don't remember what she listened to. I don't remember there ever being any TV.

You know, Mr. Steve, I don't remember as good as I used to. For example, I don't remember any of her favorite foods except that both her and Almanzo especially liked my Swiss steak. And I don't remember her saying that she had a favorite of her own books, but she did talk about her family, the whole family, but more about her sisters Mary and Grace.

Oh, Mrs. Wilder did get letters from school children, letters and letters and letters. At first, she answered each one individually, but then her eyes began to fail her. She had diabetes, and that's what caused it. Anyway, she got to where she'd just write the teacher a letter and let her read it to all the children. She even got letters from Japan.

Since then many Japanese have come to Mansfield to

visit the home. One summer [1991] they even made a movie of this place, took a helicopter and flew it all over the little town of Mansfield. They took pictures at the farm and at the school.

Mrs. Wilder and her daughter, Rose, stayed in close touch, both by telephone and by letter. I don't think Rose made it to her father's funeral. She did come down before her mother's final illness, while Mrs. Wilder was in the Springfield hospital.

> Oh, Mrs. Wilder did get letters from school children, letters and letters and letters.

One of the things we did while she was in the hospital was to take Mrs. Wilder water out of her own well. We would take her jugs of water every time we went to see her. She didn't like the Springfield water.

Mrs. Wilder was able to come home from the hospital to the house she and Mr. Wilder had built together. Not much later she died there in the home.

Weekly Visits with Laura
The Personal Recollections of Nava Austin

Nava Austin is the head librarian for the Wright County, Missouri, libraries. She presides over institutions, small though they may be, that are widely scattered. To talk to Nava Austin, you have to talk on the run.

Ms. Austin has been a librarian for the county some forty years and was present when the Mansfield library was named in honor of Laura Ingalls Wilder in September of 1951. She probably knows the history of Wright County as well as anyone.

Mrs. Wilder loved the library and loved to visit with Ms. Austin when she came to town. Mrs. Wilder's will made provision for the library, and it eventually received over $25,000 on the royalty proceeds of two of Mrs. Wilder's books.

Laura, center, at the library named in her honor

I knew Mrs. Wilder from 1951 to 1955. In 1955 her health failed, and she wasn't able to come in, as she had, every Wednesday morning for those years.

When I first got to know her, I was assistant librarian at Mansfield. She did come in every Wednesday morning to town and to the library.

There was an elderly lady in town whose name I forget—she must have been around ninety—that Mrs. Wilder would go down and have tea with. But she always said coming to the library was the highlight of her day.

Later on, she would eat lunch, most of the time at the Owens Cafe. Then Mr. Hartley would drive her down to the town of Ava because she enjoyed the scenery and the outdoors.

> She always said coming to the library was the highlight of her day.

One day, Mrs. Wilder came into the library and said, "I want you to have lunch with me. I got a surprise in the mail this morning."

"What was that?" I asked.

"Well, I got a $500 royalty check that I wasn't expecting!"

Although we didn't usually close over lunch hour, she said, "I'll go on up to the cafe and order us a shrimp dinner, and then you can come up to the cafe and take time to eat a shrimp dinner with me." So, I did.

One day Mrs. Wilder came to the library and made a

tape for me on old reel-to-reel recorders. I taped her conversation, and I taped the questions, some of which had come from children in letters they had written to her.

The sort of questions we asked her on the tape had to do with how old she was when she first began her books

Laura and the dolls made for her by Barbara Brooks

[sixty-five]. Would you care to describe each doll a little bit? Did Mary wear her bonnet better than you did and was her hair lighter than yours? [The answer was "yes" to both questions.] Would you care to tell what happened to Mary? [After Mary finished college, she lived with Ma for the rest of her life.]

We do have her doll collection, made by a Barbara Brooks in California, here at the library. They're kind of interesting. The dolls are little character dolls and show Ma sitting in her rocking chair holding baby Grace. Pa has his fiddle, and Almanzo is shown as a farmer boy who loved to fish. Mrs. Wilder felt that they were accurately made; for example, Pa had a reddish beard and the like. We do have a picture of Mrs. Wilder when she presented the dolls to us.

Laura had brown pigtails and her bonnet is not on her head. Mary, of course, has her bonnet on.

This all happened in 1953, I think, when the tape was made of her answering questions that school children had sent in about Mary and the old bulldog, Jack. She noted some differences in the dolls and the way she characteristically remembered people—Almanzo and his buffalo coat being one thing in particular.

The buffalo coat must have reminded her of some things in Almanzo's life because she talked about the book *Farmer Boy* a little bit and said that it was true and that Almanzo's house was still standing.

LAURA'S GIFTS TO HER FRIENDS

Mrs. Wilder knew she was getting pretty frail. She once said to me, "I'm giving things to people that I think they will enjoy and take care of." She gave me her family Bible, the one her mother and father gave her when she and Almanzo were married. The family Bible had clippings and obituaries in it, including one for their boy [died 1889, one month old]. I thought Rose was the only child they ever had because Mrs. Wilder herself never mentioned anything about a son.

It was a huge Bible, and there were obituaries for both her mother and father. I'd never seen a Bible like it before, and she had pictures tucked away in it. If I am not mistaken, there was a paper clipping of when she and Almanzo got married. I had the Bible until they organized the home. Then Rose, her daughter, called and said, "I'm sure that Mother didn't know these things were going to be preserved." So, I told her yes I would give it back. The Bible is on display at the home; I gave it back to Mrs. Lichty, who was curator then.

Mrs. Wilder gave away other things too, jewelry and the like, to people who had been good to her and who she thought would enjoy the items. She had quite a

> "I'm giving things to people that I think they will enjoy and take care of."

number of historical things that had been around for a long time.

She gave the library her books, which were mostly book club books. Evidently she had belonged to the Doubleday Book Club, and there may have been several other book clubs too. I would have thought there would have been more history books, but the books turned out to be mostly fiction books, mystery and western books and some bird books.

As she was giving away things, she also brought into the library Almanzo's canes, ones he had made himself, mostly from wood off the farm. One of them was made with several different kinds of wood. He had used a metal rod to run through the different pieces of cherry and oak to hold them together. Again, when the museum was set up, we gave those things back to them.

Not too long before she died, she said that I was welcome to come to her home. "Anytime you come I'll let you in, but I'm not receiving guests at all. So many people are just curious to see what I look like." She wanted to be treated just as an individual, as a person, as a friend, not as a celebrity.

THE BOOKS SHE LOVED

She talked a lot about *Little House in the Big Woods* and her childhood life. And she also talked a lot about *The Long Winter* when her father and one of the neighbors went out to try to find food. That was when they had to burn straw for fuel. But *Little House in the Big Woods* was what she talked about more than anything.

In her later years she read mostly westerns. They were paperbacks. She said, "People probably wonder why this is my type of reading, but they are easy to hold, and I just enjoy them." And she was a horse lover, a lover of the outdoors. At one point, they had raised a colt. "I did the training of it," she said. But times were hard. It finally came to the fact that they had to sell the colt to pay the taxes on their home. That broke her heart.

> But *Little House in the Big Woods* was what she talked about more than anything.

Luke Short was one of her favorite western writers, and Mrs. Wilder had a lot of those old paperbacks that looked more like magazines than the paperbacks we have today. She gave me some of those, and I still have them. Zane Grey was another favorite.

Mrs. Wilder would feel pretty embarrassed about all of the fuss being made about her today. It is just not anything she ever would have wanted. She was a very feminine little lady, but she did enjoy receiving the letters from kids.

I did take Mrs. Wilder up on her invitation to visit just one time. She wanted some books, had run out of things to read, and couldn't get out. On that day, I picked up the books she had and took her some new ones, but I really didn't sit down and visit with her. But her little kitchen was very neat. Everything was real tidy. She said reading and playing solitaire were her livelihood.

I took her mostly westerns. She wasn't feeling well, and she could hold those books in bed and read. A hardcover book was almost too heavy for her to hold, but she could relax with her westerns. I expect they reminded her somewhat of her past.

Now, I never met Almanzo, though I heard a lot about him. I was out that way the day he passed away. In fact, he had just passed away that morning, so I didn't stay or anything.

For some reason, Mrs. Wilder didn't talk about Rose much. I felt there may have been a little bit of a problem there. Her daughter didn't come often, and I don't think they were really close.

Mrs. Wilder and Rose were very different. Mrs. Wilder was very quiet and feminine, and Rose was more of the outgoing type. If Mrs. Wilder got help from Rose with her books, I never knew that.

Of course, Mrs. Wilder's books are still very popular. It is not only children; adults enjoy reading them. We have people who come back and say, "I've read them all two or three times, but I want to start them again."

When the TV show came along, I don't think it bothered people around here too much. They enjoyed *Little House on the Prairie*, but they'd comment on the difference between the show and the stories. The show was far from her books, and it was far from picturing Mrs. Wilder. But it was just a show, I'd say, based on her books.

> Of course, Mrs. Wilder's books are still very popular. It is not only children; adults enjoy reading them.

What Mrs. Wilder enjoyed doing was writing something that children would enjoy. She never figured on becoming famous. Nor was she the sort of person who felt that the old days were better. I think she was concerned about the economy and the country, but I never heard her say that she felt worried or unhappy about things either.

I don't remember her even complaining about growing older. She just accepted it as a phase of life. A lot of the time she wore a black velvet dress with a beautiful necklace. She was fond of jewelry but not overly fond. Toward the end of her years, children would write and say, "Why don't you write more books?" She would reply, "I don't want to because I would have to bring in the sad things of life."

Most of her life was spent in the present and the future. To me, she had been just a friend, a personal friend.

Volunteer for Life:
The Personal Recollections of Irene V. Lichty

Irene and her husband, L. D. Lichty, were responsible for memorializing Laura Ingalls Wilder in her chosen setting. Their volunteer-led movement kept the idea of "doing something for Mrs. Wilder" alive. With the help of Laura's daughter, Rose Wilder Lane, they were able to preserve the main artifact of Mrs. Wilder's sixty-three years in the Ozarks: her home.

Mrs. Lichty came along late in Mrs. Wilder's earthly pilgrimage, but their paths crossed by chance. Mrs. Lichty was the first curator of the Laura Ingalls Wilder Home and Museum and a driving force in its permanent establishment.

In having preserved Laura's home, Mrs. Lichty and her husband in some sense preserved Laura too. For that, thousands are thankful. Of course, time stands still for no one. Mrs. Lichty passed away in 1993, full of age and the assurance she had preserved something truly worthwhile.

The friendship between Mrs. Wilder and me just sort of happened. I first met Mrs. Wilder—and I remember it very well—at a Methodist church ladies meeting. I noticed this nice-appearing lady who seemed to be getting a lot of attention. Everyone seemed so pleased that she was there. It turned out to be Mrs. Wilder, though I didn't know who she was at the time.

In some ways, we just kind of slipped into our friendship. She and my mother were also good friends, but I was the one who really got acquainted with her. I have never really known why the Lord made it so easy for us to do this.

Now, let's see . . . Almanzo was dead, so that would have been part of it. We were in Iowa when he passed away, but when we came back we would have been available and willing to take Mrs. Wilder places.

I got to know Rose quite well. Mrs. Wilder would ring me up and say, "Rose is here. Why don't you come out?" So we were together quite a little.

Mrs. Wilder owned a car but didn't drive it, so I would drive them around. I used to take them out to eat at a popular place down Highway 60 beyond Mountain Grove. One day after we left there, I don't quite know what happened, but I screwed up a little bit in my driving. I didn't have accidents, but I must have pulled over on the shoulder. Rose didn't exactly jump; just appeared a little frightened. Mrs. Wilder herself never seemed the least bit nervous about my driving.

> In some ways, we just kind of slipped into our friendship.

At the time of Mr. Wilder's death, as I understand, she hadn't been very involved in church things. Her mode of living had changed somewhat and she wasn't so active. But during the time that I knew her, if I invited her to a meeting, she seemed happy to come. I guess she was more involved in her thinking than her activities would show.

I feel that Mrs. Wilder did have quite a few acquaintances—and many people who wanted to get acquainted with her. I don't think there was any discrimination on her part; it's just that she had only so much time and strength. She had to be a little careful.

Signing books at age eighty-four

One day I did take her into Springfield. She had been invited there to autograph books in the store. That event went on all afternoon. I knew she was getting tired, so before she got too worn out, I said to the lady running the store, "I believe that is as far as she should go."

When I left her at her home, she got out and said, "I'm quite tired but I had a good time!"

Mrs. Wilder never had television, did lots of reading, and had wide interests. She was friendly to everyone. Yet it is so often that when a person becomes famous, even their friends become a little standoffish. They may feel like this person is beyond knowing me now. I know that Mrs. Wilder would not have wanted any of her friends to feel that way.

Blue was her outstanding color, and she wore hats. Those were the days of hats. Mrs. Wilder liked most anything to eat, and she always seemed to enjoy what she had at our place, just because it was different and because she was eating with different people instead of eating alone.

Mrs. Wilder was modern in her thinking. She kept up on politics and was a staunch Democrat, though slipping a little. She would probably think it was all right for women to go outside the home to work. She was the same person when we met her, I'm sure, that she had been for years.

THE FOUNDING OF THE LAURA INGALLS WILDER
HOME AND MUSEUM

Like my getting to know Mrs. Wilder, the founding of the home just sort of happened. My husband, L. D. Lichty, was around the house, and he said to me, "Has anyone ever said anything to you about honoring Mrs. Wilder?" I said, "No, there's never been anything said about it to me."

Then I told my husband I was going to a club meeting and would mention the idea if it worked out naturally. When I did everyone seemed to pick up on it. They knew what sort of person she was and how important she was to Mansfield, but they hadn't seemed to have thought about doing anything to honor her. All I did was start a little talking and thinking about it.

In fact, that reminds me that a woman from Ava, a town which I think was a little larger than Mansfield back then, said to me, "If we had had the Wilders down in Ava, we would have done something for her before this." I thought to myself, *That's true. Ava would have.* So it took awhile for Mansfield to wake up to the opportunity.

> "Has anyone ever said anything to you about honoring Mrs. Wilder?"

None of this happened while Mrs. Wilder was living. She would have been embarrassed. For a time, things developed in a casual way. It was not the sort of thing that could be pushed.

When Rose finally understood what we wanted to do with the home, I could tell that she was pleased about it. She said, "Well, if you want to do something, I'd be glad to help." I don't think she jumped into things because, you know, in small places and in large places too, there is often someone there ready to take personal advantage.

I do recall that when the announcement was made, perhaps in the paper, that there would be an organizational meeting for anyone interested in furthering "the cause," well, the word got out some way that there was money to be distributed. That was never true. When people found out at the meeting that that wasn't so, some of them were not interested anymore.

Actually, the real opening of the house didn't take place until quite some time after Mrs. Wilder passed away. As I remember, the first time the home was open for people to look at, was when a ladies club showed some interest. So, one Sunday afternoon, people were allowed to go into the home. Enough people were there to keep an eye on things and know what was going on.

I'm afraid we never opened the upstairs. The stairway was a little treacherous. If one person went up, another person would want to also, and they wouldn't understand why you couldn't allow it.

I must say that it was some of my husband's money that took care of some things. There wasn't a lot of expense to start with; we did what came up to do. We did not charge admission at first, and that was foolish. I believe it was Rose who suggested that we had better charge admission because a lot of people were coming out of curiosity.

People came from all over the world—England,

Germany, and Japan. Most were from Europe. I don't remember anyone from the TV show ever coming by. We had a guest book and sometimes people would write their names down. We wouldn't know for sure who they were, and we didn't quiz anyone.

Friends and Neighbors
The Personal Recollections of Mrs. Iola Jones, Sheldon Jones, and Roscoe Jones

The Jones family lived just down the road from the Wilders, away from town and off to the right as you go out past the Wilder home itself. Marvin Jones moved his family there right after World War II to tackle the rough land. He always worked at a service station and did the farming on the side, a prudent thing for an Ozark farmer to do.

For the children the farm was mostly a great place to grow up and learn responsibility. The Jones boys, Sheldon and Roscoe, worked; everybody worked. Neither of the boys farm now, however. They learned that farming was good for their character but bad for their pocketbooks.

All the Joneses left the farm in 1957, though not before Marvin was a pallbearer at Mrs. Wilder's funeral. After a time in Joplin, Sheldon and Roscoe took up trucking. They live in the Springfield, Missouri, area now.

First we'll hear from Iola Jones, the boys' mother.

IOLA JONES

My husband was in the service and got home around '46. We built a house that was just east of the Wilders on the same side of the road, not toward town but away from town. E. R. Smith built a house in between ours and the Wilders', but that was much later.

The boys were over there more than I was. I was real busy, and her husband was living at that time. But it was not long after we moved there that he died.

I'd just go see her sometimes. I'd send her some cookies or something by the kids. I think one time the St. Louis paper interviewed her and said that she made cookies for the neighbor boys. But she said, "That's not what I said! I said the neighbor boys 'brought' me cookies." They were rolled sugar cookies or oatmeal cookies.

> She always had a list of little quotations or sayings or poems that she kept in her head.

When you went to visit her privately she was pretty talkative, but she wasn't that way in a crowd. She was very quiet. But to go over and visit her, no. She always had a list of little quotations or sayings or poems that she kept in her head. Sometimes I would know them; sometimes I didn't. She was just real entertaining really to visit with, and such a cute little woman.

She was always asking about my boys, Sheldon and

Roscoe. She didn't think they would ever do anything bad. One time when I was over she told me, "Sheldon will be over here and I will think: *It must be Sheldon that I love the best.* Then, in a day or so, Roscoe will come and then I'll think: *Oh, no. It must be Roscoe that I love the best.*" She really was crazy about the boys.

Both of them did work for her in and around the house. Sheldon was laughing about it the other night, saying he'd work all day raking the gravel in the driveway and tending to the grass. At the end of the day, Sheldon said, "I got my quarter!" (When Mrs. Wilder grew up, a quarter was a lot of money.)

When the boys would visit her, they were so interested in life back then, they would ask her all kinds of questions about life in her books. She loved to talk about that, of course. And they liked to hear it.

The teacher used to read these books at school, and I used to read [them to the boys] a lot after chores were done, supper was over, and the dishes were done and the fire was revved up for the evening.

I remember one night they brought home a book that the teacher had already read to them. I hadn't read the book, and the boys were sitting on either side of me. I said, "Now, I'm going to finish this one chapter, and you go to bed." But it was kind of exciting, so I too wanted to see what happened next. "Just one more chapter, just one more," the boys said.

Then one of them started to say what was going to happen in the chapter we were reading, and the other one said, "Oh, let Mother be surprised." "You've already read this!" I said. "Oh, yes." But those books were so interesting they wanted me to read, read, read. Once she asked the boys which one was their favorite. Sheldon liked *Farmer Boy*, so she gave him that autographed for Christmas. Roscoe liked *The Long Winter*, and she gave him that. I wish we could have afforded a complete set for both of them, but we couldn't afford that. They must have been $2.75 a book.

> Those books were so interesting they wanted me to read, read, read.

Just south of the Wilder house is a spring, and terrapins [turtles] used to come up from this spring to the back porch where the screen came down way low. In the evenings those terrapins got so that they would line up and look in. Then Mrs. Wilder would fix bread in milk and feed them as they stretched out their necks. I've never seen anything like it.

Of course, they had their own animals—milk goats. And they were always able to keep them in. In fact, the Wilder fence came right up to our yard, and our kids would feed the goats. I used to warn them that the one billy goat would come over that fence after them, but it never did.

Mrs. Wilder was always doing things for people, sending them things, like birthday cards she would write to you. I would send her some of my light bread, homemade bread made with regular flour. I don't think they had whole-wheat flour back then. If they did, we didn't use it.

She'd also eat an awful lot of fruit. She believed in eating the right things. I remember being there when they brought the groceries in, lots of grapefruit, bananas, and oranges, and she'd cook. She'd make soup.

So far as dress goes, she dressed old-fashion-like. She had nice clothes, but they were clothes she had had a long time. When she went to church, she was real old-fashioned, lace around her neck. I remember she had one dark maroon velvet dress, which she wore at the library dedication when it was named after her. I've got a napkin from that time with the date written on it.

Of course, she had done sewing earlier in her life, but at the time I knew her, she didn't do that. Instead, she read a lot and had lots of mail.

Sometimes the mail would get to be too much and she'd have her hands full. Sometimes Roscoe would help her with it, sometimes Sheldon. At her age, I don't think she could respond to it all.

She spent a lot of time just sitting in a chair right there by the dining room table. We'd find her there when we went over.

Once in a while we would sit on the swing on the porch, but not too often. When she wanted to show you something, she would jump right up and take off. She didn't have arthritis, and she got around fast.

She used to talk about her family of long ago. Especially I remember her talking about the sister who was blind. That was Mary. And she talked about how she would make word pictures for Mary so she could "see." She was a special companion to Mary and had lots of feeling for her.

Mary's organ was there in the home, but I don't know whether she played it or not.

Mrs. Wilder had a good sense of humor and lots of wisdom, really; and she put it across in such an interesting way. She had been quite active in her church. In fact, she went to church with me quite a lot, which was a pickup in her activity because before that she hadn't been going. You see, I don't think she ever drove, so I think Almanzo's death kept her in.

> Mrs. Wilder had a good sense of humor and lots of wisdom, really; and she put it across in such an interesting way.

She did talk about spiritual things, and we went together to the Methodist Church where she had always gone. I can remember her telling me one time that she had memorized a book of the Bible, but I don't remember which one. She just didn't talk about herself a lot.

I would say that Rose was not the same type of person as her mother. Of course, she had traveled a lot and was real interesting to visit with. She'd come from Danbury, Connecticut, to visit her mother, but she didn't stay very long. I remember Mrs. Wilder as being sort of stylish, and her hair was gray and always fixed up. By comparison Rose didn't seem that refined.

I am sure Mrs. Wilder had a lot of money. Sheldon was saying to me that one time when he was over there helping with the stacks of mail, she remarked that she needed to go to the bank; the money had gotten to be a chore. There was about $6,000 on that table.

When we visited the Home, the place seemed pretty much the same except that there were fewer trees, and they had changed the driveway. When Mrs. Wilder died, my husband was a pallbearer. You know, I have the little memorial of her funeral service, but I don't even remember the hymns that we sang. That was a long time ago.

SHELDON JONES

Sheldon Jones picks up where his mother has left off. He had only recently been reminded of Mrs. Wilder. He too had been to the Home and Museum but had come away dissatisfied. His memory is almost too good, and he is disquieted about inaccuracies that tend to crop up when people who never knew Mrs. Wilder attempt to explain how they lived or, specifically, how Mrs. Wilder lived toward the end of her life.

Though he was only a young boy during Mrs. Wilder's later years, he had a keen eye for details that he now shares with enthusiasm and obvious enjoyment. It takes little prompting for him to remember those days.

Only last night, I was talking about working for her. And if I wasn't working for her, I'd run by and see about her. You see, until Almanzo died they were pretty much loners. In fact, I never saw him, not one time to speak of. He must have been sort of like her dad. You might be twenty miles away, but you were still too close. He didn't deal with people; at that time he had little to do with them. Now she, Mrs. Wilder, was quite a lady.

> Now she, Mrs. Wilder, was quite a lady.

I really got to going over there after he died. Then she needed help. But the house really wasn't open for visitors. There were always people coming by in the summertime wanting to meet her. I don't know how many times I'd be working in the yard when I'd have to make a run for the back door to get between visitors and the house.

They'd say, "We want to meet Mrs. Wilder." They'd

come from Iowa, Nebraska, and, of course, Missouri and Kansas and way-off states and even foreign countries. And I'd have to say, "No, no, no. It's not that she is uppity or anything, but she won't be coming to the door; she won't meet you. It's not that she's so important or nothing, but the reason I am here is this is as far as it goes."

I told a lot of people that. You know, a kid standing there telling you that, wouldn't you like to knock him down? But I felt like I was protecting her. I knew that was what she wanted because there would be times when people would come, and she'd be at the door herself saying, "Thanks for coming, but no. . . ."

At that time, she just didn't want to get out much. I think Ma and I and Roscoe and Virginia Hartley and a few others were about the only ones she saw.

So, I took her the mail and mowed the yard with a power mower. Actually, there were push mowers for quite a while. I mowed her yard and the yard of the folks that had bought land out there from her.

I was out there raking one day during the fall when it was extremely windy. I was battling like crazy when she came out and said, "Aren't you fighting it? We'll consider it two-days' work."

I was telling Mom last night that the driveway is all changed now. It made a sweeping circle, then came down to the road, the opposite of the way it is now. But I'd go down and rake that gravel because it would wash out.

She wanted it raked in such a way that the gravel would be heaped back where it belonged. She wanted sort of a mound of gravel so it wouldn't wash the driveway away.

Sometimes that is about all I got done there. Then I would put up the tools. She was a real stickler for putting up the tools exactly where Almanzo had hung them, I suppose because they were placed right there by him and everything was hung up. He spent his lifetime taking care of his tools, and she knew where they went.

Mrs. Wilder gave me a quarter for that work. That was big money for a kid. I imagine when she was a kid you'd work maybe for a penny, and she must have pinched pennies all her life.

Mrs. Wilder probably didn't realize what she had. I don't know what kind of money they had before the books, but they must have lived modestly, simply. I'm sure he was an ace farmer from what I gathered from her. But she had a big table maybe three and a half feet across. No, maybe not that big. But I'd be there to visit her, and there would be a pile of money on the table, checks and money, maybe four inches high.

> Mrs. Wilder gave me a quarter for that work. That was big money for a kid.

Why she had the money I don't know. Royalties wouldn't have come that way; but if she was going to write me something, she'd push that pile back out of the way. It was aggravating; money was a nuisance. She told my brother one time, "This must get to the bank; this is such an aggravation!" I suppose Hartley could have taken her to town. But she didn't leave; she didn't get out much.

Once I went out to the house with my daughter, who was four or five. And this young lady, maybe she was from New York or Pennsylvania or something, led us around; and she had a little story, but it was all wrong from what I remembered. The more she talked, the more irritable I got.

Finally, she came to Mrs. Wilder's parlor where she had kept all her books, and she said, "This is where Mrs. Wilder entertained all her guests." Then I said, "No, young lady. That is not right. This room was kept closed."

You see, that parlor was kept dark, never used. Many a time I would go in there during the winter and take all the books out and lay them around and turn on electric heaters to dry them out. It was damp in there and dark, and it was never heated.

The young lady was taken aback, but said maybe Mrs. Wilder could have entertained guests there. Of course, I don't know about the years before we knew her as to what she did. But I interrupted at another point and said, "No, no. There's not a word of truth to that." So one guy said, "Did you know her?"

I said, "I worked for her when I was a kid for several

years. During the summertime my brother and I would go in here and move these heavy old drapes and open the windows, and it would air out all day. The doors would be opened up, everything. And then before I left that evening the windows would be closed, the drapes pulled, and the door closed. It stayed dark, and she never went in there."

> I was always asking her about her books and what kind of life she led.

That was the room that had the fireplace. She lived basically in the dining room, kitchen, and bedroom. That was it because I remember seeing her once in that little screened-in porch that is just off the dining room. Mrs. Wilder and Mom used to go out there and sit, and one day I saw them there. I remember it because it was so unusual to see anybody there.

Mainly the house was the kitchen, the dining room, and the bedroom. That's all the house she used. It was a dark place, always dark. In fact, the only time I ever remember even seeing Mr. Wilder was while we were bailing hay. We hayed all around that place, and he didn't even speak then. I couldn't tell you what he looked like because he mostly stayed in the house too.

I don't think Mrs. Wilder realized what she had done, what she had created in her books. I think she was just writing down memories at the time, just sketching, just thinking about the past. For somebody to really get excited about it—how did she put that to me one time? "What do you see in them?" she asked.

My gosh! I would have loved to live in those times!

I was always asking her about her books and what kind of life she led. She was truthful in her books, but she was always cautious about who she named and how she showed them. I remember her talking about that mean girl, Nellie. Of course, that wasn't her real name, but I remember Mrs. Wilder saying that she didn't put her down nearly as mean as she was.

When she talked about Pa, Ma, and Mary, it was pretty much in line with the books. Her dad's attitude was, if he could see smoke coming from a chimney, he didn't have to see the chimney. People were too close; they'd move on. I remember she mentioned the moving.

Mrs. Wilder thought her bulldog, an old boxer with some black color around one eye, was the greatest thing that walked around on four legs. He had the rule of the place. You'd come in the house, and he'd come out of the bedroom and go straight upstairs from the kitchen, straight up. It was some sort of escape in case of fire.

If the dog didn't want to bother with you, he never got up. He just lay there in a corner. But a lot of times that sucker would come up slobbering and lay his head right in your lap! That dog got killed on the highway that runs by the place. It really hurt Mrs. Wilder bad.

> Mrs. Wilder thought her bulldog, an old boxer with some black color around one eye, was the greatest thing that walked around on four legs. He had the rule of the place.

One time I was sitting there with Mrs. Wilder after dark. I liked most animals, and she had a big cat that was sitting on my lap. Mrs. Wilder was sitting over at the table where she always sat. I was petting the cat, playing with him, and I got to teasing him. I didn't think Mrs. Wilder could see me. The cat was sitting in my lap and I would blow in his face. You know how they don't like that. He'd lay back his ears, and snarl at me, just mad enough to kill, and then I'd pet him and it would be over with. Then I'd go do it to him again.

I tell you, all of a sudden, that old tom cat took a swipe at me and jumped off my lap. I said, "What's the matter, cat?" She said, "He wouldn't do that if you wouldn't pick on him." She'd seen it all!

Mrs. Wilder was something. She was a real lady, absolutely a real lady.

ROSCOE JONES
Roscoe Jones runs a trucking company and a mobile phone is ever with him. Although running such an operation does call for travel, he is surprised by how seldom he goes down

to Mansfield, which is about fifty miles east of Springfield where he now lives.

Roscoe was nine years old when Almanzo died. Both of the Jones "boys" have a great capacity for recalling detail, but they wish they remembered more of their neighbor. To them, she was just that—very interesting to talk to and convenient to do odd jobs for, but not a celebrity. That would have been a foreign term to them. They make clear that Mrs. Wilder never considered herself a celebrity either and avoided the limelight if at all possible.

Whereas Sheldon has spoken with more of a narrative to his reminiscences, Roscoe's style is more clipped and direct, possibly because I talked with him over lunch in the midst of a rushed day.

Pretty much what Sheldon and I did for her was seasonal chores. When it started turning cold, she always wanted a bale of straw broken and put back under the areas of the house to close the vents to make it airtight.

> She used to tell us the same stories she wrote about in her books.

That was it basically. Sometimes she would have something in the house to move. One day she called me and asked me to come over and move some stuff for her. At that time, she gave me her old typewriter, which I still have. I hauled it home on my motor scooter.

Really we didn't get to know Mrs. Wilder until Mr. Wilder died. As boys we would have never gone up there on our own because he seemed like a grouchy old man. I do remember seeing him a few times. He would come out into the yard when we would drive up.

When he died I began mowing her yard. We always had a power mower, but you had to push it. It was a big, big job.

Really, Mrs. Wilder was a very, very kind person and a real sweet lady. She used to call and have us pick up her mail when she couldn't do it. That driveway must have been rather steep to her.

Sometimes she just wanted to visit with someone. She used to tell us the same stories she wrote about in her books. Then she'd say, "Well, now this is the way this story actually happened." She would say that some of the book, I forget the term she used, was more "flowery" or something to "jazz it up," although I am certain she wouldn't use that term.

I don't remember her ever saying that she had a favorite story. She talked very fondly of her family and about all of the hard times they had gone through.

No, she never went through the house to point out any items of special interest. I do recall being fascinated by some sort of apparatus she had in her library. It had a light with a colored lens of some sort on it that was used to dry out books or keep down the humidity level. I mentioned that when I was down at the home a few years ago, but no one else seemed to know about it.

I don't think Mrs. Wilder had too much of a fancy for fine furnishings. In fact, I don't ever remember her talking about things.

But she liked to talk, and she had a sense of humor; she surely did. When she received candy in the mail, I don't know where it came from, maybe the publisher, she would have Sheldon and me over. She would get boxes of chocolates and that was sort of a rare thing for us at that time.

In dress, Mrs. Wilder was old-fashioned. She wore long dresses around the house with a sweater and maybe a shawl and laced-up boots. Nothing fancy. Actually, she didn't even have a couch in the room where the stove was. She sat in a rocking chair, and there may have been a side chair or two, just straight wooden chairs.

> She talked very fondly of her family and about all of the hard times they had gone through.

Possibly Mr. Wilder made the chairs. I don't know. I am sure that Mrs. Wilder did not sell off his tools. I don't remember if they sold them off after she died or not.

Mr. Wilder made toy wagons the size of coaster wagons.

His were quite unique because the bed of the wagon was made to look more like that of a full-sized wagon. It had larger wheels on the rear than on the front. These wagons were always fascinating to me, and I have no idea what became of them. Of course, the old shop is gone, but I've been told by other people that he was quite a handyman. I don't know why or for whom he made those wagons.

Virginia Hartley was probably her closest friend of long-standing. Virginia's father-in-law had a taxi service and I do remember him coming out whenever the Wilders wanted to go someplace. I remember it was a green Oldsmobile.

However, she did come to rely on Mother quite a bit and developed a fairly close relationship with her in the years we lived there. And Mother provided a ride for her to get started going back to church. Before that I don't think she had been there for years. She did come to feel free to call Mother for things she might need. Yes, they were fairly close.

Mother and daughter were not so close, I think. I remember meeting Rose on two or three occasions, and she was there for her mother's funeral. Rose would come to visit for a week or two at a time, and she wasn't nearly as easy to visit with as her mother because she seemed so brash.

I'm not sure they got along too well. They seemed to tolerate each other while Rose visited. I even remember Mrs. Wilder saying that she was not looking forward to her upcoming visit with Rose.

FOUR

MOTHER AND
DAUGHTER

*"Something magic happened when they linked
up as a team, because what started out as a simple
set of stories of long ago ended up as a complex
but unified saga of American family life."*

Laura and Rose

Now Rose takes center stage—Rose, the famous and only daughter of Laura Ingalls Wilder. Once a well-known writer, she authored two best-selling books in the 1930s: *Let the Hurricane Roar*, a book based on the pioneering of Charles and Caroline Ingalls in Minnesota in fictionalized form, and *Free Land*, a fictional account of Laura and Almanzo's pioneering in South Dakota.

To some students of the books written by Laura and her daughter, Rose was the only real writer in the family, with hundreds of articles, essays, and short stories to her credit.

Yet in terms of popular reputation, by the late 1940s

Rose Wilder Lane became known more as the daughter of Laura Ingalls Wilder than as a celebrated novelist in her own right. Instead, Rose became more political and didactic as she devoted her time to the promotion of libertarianism through her books and essays. (To Rose, the greatest amount of personal freedom coupled with the greatest amount of self-sufficiency equaled a life true to American pioneer history and ideals.)

> Rose Wilder Lane became known more as the daughter of Laura Ingalls Wilder than as a celebrated novelist in her own right.

While Rose was writing philosophy, Laura was credited with creating a fascinating personal account of America's history through the adventures of her memorable family. Her daughter's philosophical books, no matter how heartfelt, could not compete. Rose began to sink into something like literary oblivion.

This must have been a difficult turn of events for both women. And it did not help much that Rose's presence in her own hometown had worn thin too. Mansfield residents had become horrified when it seemed they turned up as characters in one of her books, *Old Home Town*. Town folk also found Rose outspoken, opinionated, and abrasive when women were still supposed to be more like Laura Ingalls Wilder: refined, pleasant, and soft-spoken.

Rose, on a walking tour in France

Mrs. Wilder did the best she could with what must have been an increasingly awkward situation. She was always quick to say that her daughter was the real writer in the family; she rightly boasted of Rose's considerable accomplishments as only she could know, for the evidence does show that Laura needed the editorial talents of her daughter as the series progressed.

The truth is, Rose's greatest work was what she did for her mother. Something magic happened when they linked up as a team, because what started out as a simple set of stories of long ago ended up as a complex but unified saga of American family life.

Not all of the genius was on Rose's side. Mother and daughter worked together.

Rose played a key part in the development of the series, but she was only a part of the equation. It is important that both mother and daughter get credit for the timeless appeal of Laura's stories.

Mother and Daughter
The Personal Recollections of Tom Carnall
and Alvie Turner

All throughout her life, it seems that Rose struck many Mansfield people as being rough and abrasive, while they regarded Mrs. Wilder as refined and polished. No doubt others will continue a quest for the correct literary assessment of Rose, but a balanced character assessment need not undergo such a debate; for as the following interviews show, Rose certainly did have her admirers too. And if adults were not always comfortable with this strong-willed woman, at least some others saw quite a different side to her personality. They remember her as the most fascinating person they ever met, and the Turner boys, John and Alvie, had much to be thankful for in Rose's friendship, as you will see. Let's begin with the memories of their good friend Tom Carnall.

TOM CARNALL

Tom Carnall is mayor of Sparta, Missouri, and was a close friend of the Turners. John and Alvie Turner were young boys who came to live with Rose shortly after their parents died. They were of high school age, and Mr. Carnall recalls quite a few afternoons and evenings spent at Rose's place.

My first association with any of these people who visited Rose or who lived at her home was in 1934. Two boys were living there named John and Al Turner. John could have been just barely fifteen and Al was about sixteen and I was about seventeen years old: freshman, sophomore, and junior in high school. The whole graduating class of 1936 had only thirteen students! The whole school, grades 1–12, may have had 250 students, in one two-story building.

John and Alvie came from Douglas County just south of Wright County. Their grandfather was sheriff there, and they had one sister that I knew about. But their parents were dead, to my remembrance. My folks' property adjoined Rose's parents' property. . . .

Anyway, I got to know the boys because I lived so close. We got acquainted as the school year began in '34, and I would go out to their home periodically. Well, almost each day we'd walk home for lunch out there to her house. Since we had an hour for lunch, we would walk out there three-quarters of a mile.

Now, as I recall, Corinne Murray would take care of the lunch. She was Rose's housekeeper, companion, and driver, and Corinne worked out there almost all the time; but her husband worked in town. Corinne was a real good cook, and she did a real good job of taking care of Rose's property. That left Rose time for her work.

Periodically, Rose would just isolate herself and write. She would retire to the upstairs of this two-story home and begin working. She didn't want to be bothered when she was writing, so we knew to be quiet whenever she was upstairs. Sometimes she might not come down for days on end; you wouldn't see her for maybe two or three weeks. I think her most famous book was *Let the Hurricane Roar*; and although I didn't read it, I know my father liked it.

Once in a while, when she knew we were there, she'd come down and say hi to us. Maybe she would get a cup of coffee and walk around a little bit, but then she'd go right back to work. I'd say she was a very even-tempered, good-natured old lady. That's how I saw her then, as an elderly lady. [Rose would have been in her late forties.]

Although she didn't eat with us, I do remember a comical incident about lunch. Rose and Corinne were gone that day, and we came in to get something to eat. We went to the refrigerator and found what we thought was a pretty good batch of minced ham. We made sandwiches right quick, drank a couple of glasses of milk, and went on back to school.

That evening, I went back with John and Al to play for a while before I went home. When we went inside, Corinne asked, "Did you boys eat that dog food that was in the refrigerator?"

"Dog food! No, we didn't eat any dog food. We had some of that minced ham."

"My goodness," she said, "that wasn't minced ham; that was dog food I put in there."

Those dog food sandwiches didn't bother us at all.

Rose started these parties to get John and Al better acquainted with the other kids in town. We are not talking about a large group of people, but it got to be a regular thing. She even had a dance pavilion built by a real good carpenter named Bruce Prock who lived just across the road on some old Wilder land that was bisected by Highway 60, which runs past the house.

My remembrance is that the dance pavilion was probably about thirty feet square and was screened in, with glass windows so it could be closed up in the wintertime. It had a nice dance floor, good lights, and heating. There would be parties there about every Friday or Saturday night. If there was a ball game on Friday night, then the party was on Saturday. She was really interested in young people, and the parties were always chaperoned. They usually ran from about seven o'clock until about eleven; something like that.

The refreshments would typically be stuff like lemonade and popcorn. There was no alcohol, no smoking, nothing like that at that time. She didn't approve of that at all.

Sometimes it was just too cold to dance, and we'd come into the house and go to the west room where the big fireplace is. The kids would have popcorn and soda pop, and Rose would tell true stories from her life.

> Rose was a master storyteller. She could absolutely enthrall you by the fascinating way she could describe a situation and get you right into it.

Now, Rose was a master storyteller. She could absolutely enthrall you by the fascinating way she could describe a situation and get you right into it. One night I happened to turn around while she was talking and looked at the group. There must have been twenty of us. It was the first time I ever saw high school kids so interested in a thing that a lot of them had their mouths open like little kids of five and six years old. They were so enthralled by this story that they didn't even realize what their facial expressions were!

Generally, she told adventure stories. For example, she was a great lover of Albania and had been there, I think, shortly after World War I. She became really attached to the people and just fell in love with the country, so many of her tales were about Albania and their striving for liberty. Now, I understood that she may have gone back there shortly before World War II or even during World War II to help these people in their fight against Germany. Maybe she was even in the underground, but I never knew that to be true, for sure. It was just worded around. So far as I know, she never read any of her writings to us.

She was quite busy all of the time, but you never did know what she was writing. Eventually, she moved to Columbia to the Tiger Hotel where she rented a rather large apartment. She was doing research, I believe, and Al went up there to go to the university.

In the spring of the year I graduated, 1936, she told me that if I wanted to go to college, and if I'd go work and make enough to pay my tuition, she would furnish me a place to stay up there. So that fall I stayed with Al and went to school one semester. That was all I got to go.

We didn't see much of Mr. and Mrs. Wilder. My stepfather worked with Almanzo doing repair work, fences, and things like that. Almanzo was a rather small man. I'd say he was about 5' 4", best I can remember. And he had a club foot; it seems to me it was his left one. But he was not like the TV guy, the big strong man. At least not at that time, he wasn't.

Now, Laura was the boss of the place, no question about that in anybody's mind. She ramrodded the whole thing. Yet she was very easy to get along with, congenial and all. But whenever she told Almanzo to do something, she meant it.

I had no idea she was writing too, but then she would have been communicating more with people like my mother, Violet Carnall. Seemingly, Mrs. Wilder didn't have a great lot of friends. They didn't associate with people in town a lot and didn't do much socializing.

> Now, Laura was the boss of the place, no question about that in anybody's mind.

I guess Almanzo was still doing a little farming. They ran some cattle at that time and had a hired man to work for them, probably a pretty good number of cattle for an old Missouri farm.

Now, Laura and my mother visited quite regularly, and I remember my mother telling me, after Laura began to write and sell books, that Mrs. Wilder had come over and visited with her one afternoon and wanted to know if my mother thought anybody would be interested in her life story, written for children. My mother encouraged her to write the book and said she thought it would be quite successful. Mother always felt good that she had encouraged Laura because of the success she did have.

I can remember only one time that Mr. and Mrs. Wilder ever came to any of our parties. They were over there visiting one evening when the kids started gathering in. I remember Rose saying to her mother, "Why don't you just stay and visit awhile. The kids will all be here soon, and we will have popcorn and sandwiches in a little bit."

"Oh, no. We don't want to bother anybody," they said.

"Oh, Mamma, you won't bother anybody; the kids would like to see you anyway," Rose said.

That was the only time I ever remember them staying. They enjoyed it. I remember Almanzo sitting over there talking with some of the girls. He was stomping his foot in time to the music. I don't know whether Mrs. Wilder approved of that, but at least he was enjoying it. . . .

ALVIE TURNER

Throughout her life Rose displayed an unusual generosity toward those in need. She seemed to believe that social security worked best when individuals met other individuals' needs. Rose had a way of "adopting" people, and when two boys living in the tough circumstances of the depression came along, she didn't hesitate to keep them.

John and I came to be with Rose this way. Our folks had died about a year apart, so we were taken in by my uncle in Ava, Missouri. He was the sheriff, but he also ran the waterworks. He always carried two jobs; had to in those days to keep ahead with a family.

Well, John wasn't happy there—he was two years

younger than me—he ran off. He would have been all of twelve or a little older, I guess, and the next thing we heard of him was that some folks from Ava had seen him in Mansfield at a ball game.

Apparently, he stopped by Mrs. Lane's house one day and wanted to do some work for food, and she said she had plenty of work. She liked his work and fixed a place in the garage for him to sleep. After that she started him to high school. That's when people from Ava found out that my brother was up there.

Anyway, she felt that he needed to have somebody with him, so unbeknownst to me, she talked to my uncle about my going up there too. He said it would be fine with him, so he talked with me about it. Whatever I wanted to do would be okay, he said. He said that times were hard, and he didn't think he could put me through high school, at least not right then anyway.

My uncle said, "You can stay with me or go with her, but I think it would be better if you go with her because she'll put you through high school." So we both went to high school there in Mansfield. That was for three years.

It was fun living with Mrs. Lane. She supported us all the time in whatever we did. We did a lot of "experiments." If we were interested in electronics, she'd finance some of our little projects, tubes and things.

Of course, we did have chores. We did the yard work,

milked the cow, checked the coal furnace, which was underneath the garage where today's museum bookstore is now, and kept the hot water radiators going. The clinkers had to be cleaned out and taken away.

The other help on the place was Corinne Murray, who lived there all the time and did the housecleaning, the grocery buying, and the cooking. Her husband ran a laundry in town, but he stayed in town all the time. Once in a while he would be out for supper, very seldom though.

Mrs. Lane went to her typewriter just like a person goes to work, for long hours. But she never talked about what she was working on that I remember. I never remember hearing her or her mother talk about writing. Probably if I'd had my head up I might have, but I was only about sixteen or seventeen.

Mrs. Wilder was the prettiest old woman I ever saw. But the Wilders didn't get out much, not after dark anyway. Almanzo did chores around the house and kept the fences mended. We had one cow. I don't know if he ever milked the cow or not. We kept it across the road in a barn. We didn't have pets though; Rose was not a pet person.

I was never over at the Wilder place very much. If I had known then what I know now, I'd have spent a lot of time over there.

Really, Mrs. Lane became our family. It went great. She took care of whatever we needed. We bought our clothes from the Montgomery Ward catalog and went on trips to Joplin or Springfield in her Nash. Corinne did the driving and took us to ball games and the like.

Recently I read where Rose had been pinching pennies all that time. I didn't know anything about that. If we needed a shirt, we got a shirt. If she thought we needed anything, we got it. In the wintertime, she bought oranges. "Don't eat all this candy," she'd say. We'd eat all the oranges we could. She bought them by the case.

Mrs. Lane started the kids coming out. She wanted to do something, so she started a French class, a one-hour lesson a week. Sometimes we would have twenty or so come out. She'd teach for an hour and then we'd dance for an hour.

> Mrs. Wilder was the prettiest old woman I ever saw.

You know, she spoke six languages. She must have picked them up just like that. She was fluent in Albanian, French, German, though not so good, and Italian and Greek. She was in Greece a good long while. She said one time that the king of Greece proposed to her; the king of Albania also proposed. But she didn't have any men in her life when I knew her.

Anyway, we danced for an hour, big band music of the day. Glenn Miller, Benny Goodman, all those guys. I believe there was some jitterbugging, but once in a while a friend would come up from Ava. He played the fiddle, and we would get together with him and try square dancing. His dad taught him, and he was good.

I believe Mrs. Wilder and Mrs. Lane may have visited each other as often as three times a week, but this usually would be while we were at school. A lot of times Mrs. Lane would say, "I had tea with Mother this afternoon." She didn't discuss her work; didn't discuss her mother's work.

Mrs. Lane was really something though. She could sure tell stories. We'd have regular meals if we weren't going anywhere. Then supper was a time when we'd sit and listen to her tell stories. She'd tell stories every night if we were there.

> Supper was a time when we'd sit and listen to her tell stories. She'd tell stories every night if we were there.

The stories could be about whatever you wanted.

"You want a scary story tonight?"

"Yeah," we'd say.

Or it might be a mystery story. She told a lot of stuff about her life as a story, a lot about her travels.

The place is pretty much today as I remember it back then, but the driveway looped in a circle by the kitchen door. And we got our water from a well located about five feet from the back porch. She had an electric pump.

The furniture is pretty much as I remember it, but there wasn't the organ. I never saw her play a musical instrument. Jack and I fooled with the guitar.

Also the wood stove wasn't there either. That's been put there for looks. Mrs. Lane had a modern stove.

Our senior year, Mrs. Lane moved her residence to the Tiger Hotel in Columbia, Missouri. That was about 1936, I think. I went up there to University High School and graduated. She sent John to the New Mexico Military Institute in Roswell, New Mexico. For a graduation present, she sent us both to Europe.

You see, I took a friend with me from high school—he financed his part. We hitchhiked up to Schenectady, New York, and John and his friend, a college student, rode the bus up there. Then from there we went on to Montreal, the four of us, and got on a boat. It was about $100 for each of us for the boat. I was in Europe for about three months, and it cost $300. Mrs. Lane paid all that.

After the trip to Europe, I tried college for a semester, but it didn't work out, so I went to work somewhere. We didn't write a lot; we sent Christmas cards and stuff like that. John stayed with her a long time, but I didn't keep in touch with him either. I don't write.

The most memorable thing about staying with Mrs. Lane was that we had fun. She had an outgoing personality, and she made it fun for us.

FIVE

UNSOLVED MYSTERIES

"There is the . . . problem of wanting the really 'good' stories to be true so you can use them. You want them to have really happened, but for one reason or another you are not sure."

Unsolved Mysteries

Mark Twain once observed that as he grew older his memory became better and better until it was so finely honed he could remember things that never happened! But people who want to know about the remarkable Mrs. Laura Ingalls Wilder want to know what really happened.

That's the problem. We are all a bit like Mark Twain, and in a book of this nature, there is the additional problem of wanting the really "good" stories to be true so you can use them. You want them to have really happened, but for one reason or another you are not sure.

So I have decided to present the following facts, suppositions, and queries. I hope that if some reader knows the answer to any of the following questions, I shall hear from him or her.

MYSTERY NUMBER ONE: LAURA'S CAVE

This isn't a buried treasure story; but there are literally dozens of such stories from the Ozarks. They commence with the days of the Conquistadors and most relate how some Indian of the region passed on to an early settler the approximate location of Spanish treasure, which, of course, never has been found but presumably remains lost in one of the thousands of Ozark caverns speckling the entire region.

Laura's cave story comes about through a recollection of Aleene Kindel of Clarion, Pennsylvania. Aleene didn't know Mrs. Wilder personally, but she did do a lot of nursing home visitation in Springfield, Missouri. One day in her visitations she met a woman who had been in the hospital with Mrs. Wilder when she was very sick toward the end of her life.

Mrs. Wilder shared with her roommate some of the experiences of her past and mentioned that early in her arrival in the Ozarks she and Almanzo and Rose had had to tough out part of a winter in a cave (perhaps the unimproved log house on the Wilders' newly bought farm was not warm enough for the coldest days of the year?).

This story is all plausible enough, especially when you consider that Mrs. Wilder did spend part of her growing-up years underground, as she recounts in *On the Banks of Plum Creek*. The story does have a confusing element, however, because Aleene remembers her elderly friend as saying that the location of the cave was Pine Top (not on a map) near Hollister, Missouri (very definitely on the map but nowhere near where Mrs. Wilder is supposed to have ever lived).

I became inclined to discount the story until I talked with James V. Lichty, a grandson of Irene Lichty. Mr. Lichty had spent a summer at the Wilder home doing work for his grandmother. In the course of the summer, becoming acquainted with Wilder lore, he discovered that there is indeed a cave below the bluff of a hill, protected from the winds, which was part of the old Wilder property. It would have served nicely as winter protection. (The cave is not part of the home-site now and is not available to the public.) Aleene mentions that Mrs. Wilder supposedly did some of her cooking in the cave but that it was only a temporary shelter.

Naturally, confirming evidence on this story is hard to come by, but perhaps there is someone, still unknown to me, around Mansfield or Hartville who could confirm or disprove it.

MYSTERY NUMBER TWO: WHAT BECAME OF THE ARTIFACTS,
OR WHERE IS MARY'S ORGAN?

There is a beautiful organ in the Rocky Ridge farmhouse of Almanzo and Laura Wilder, but it is not Mary's so far as can be ascertained. Where, then, is Mary's famous organ? It would seem an impossible artifact to lose or to be destroyed, but it is surely lost.

Readers of the indispensable *Laura Ingalls Wilder Lore* newsletter know that the family possessions of the Ingallses were dispersed at the deaths of various family members. (Indeed, it is from the *Lore* that we learn that the organ is not Mary's.) Small items that could be easily shipped were more likely to be saved than larger items that wouldn't be used.

Carrie Ingalls Swanzey, the last surviving Ingalls daughter to live in South Dakota, kept what she could, dispersed what she could, and sold the rest. When she herself died, in 1946, even more material was scattered.

The organ presently in the Wilder home in Mansfield is artifactual in that it is like the organ Mary might have used and has long been associated with the home, but its origin is something of a mystery. Mrs. Wilder herself did not play. "The only musical instrument I can play is the phonograph," she once wrote. Yet the current organ has been in the Wilder home for some years. Apparently, what keeps it from being the organ everyone wants it to be is the manufacture date and lack of any confirming evidence as to when it first appeared and from where.

But Mary's organ is only one item. Almanzo had an entire shop of prized hand tools with which he made his canes, small wagons, and furniture for the home. The fact that Mr. Wilder couldn't part with his tools kept him from selling the farm and moving into one of the Seals's apartments.

Apparently, the toolshed remained intact until Laura died and then . . . who knows? It would have been a wonderful display.

MYSTERY NUMBER THREE: HOW DID LAURA REALLY COME TO WRITE HER PIONEER SAGA?

With many famous events that become part of our recent history, some who have heard of an event also claim to have been there. So it is with just where, when, and how Mrs. Wilder decided to do her pioneer saga. Rose has generally been given credit for urging her mother to put her stories down on paper. Indeed, the evidence seems unquestionable that Rose did as has been recorded.

But the evidence also seems unquestionable that the idea of doing some writing of her own was Mrs. Wilder's from very early on. Indeed, she had been writing for children for many years.

Yet Mansfield residents remember just as clearly that Mrs. Wilder was discussing with them the possibility of writing about her childhood, with daughter Rose only being a marginal factor in the beginning as Mrs. Wilder sought her neighbors' advice as to what she should do.

There are enough different versions of the beginnings of the series to make it clear that the idea did not come full-blown overnight to anyone. Perhaps it is the case, as in all good things, that how the good fortune came about is not as important as that circumstances all came together. Mrs. Wilder and her publisher only foresaw one book, but public demand took care of the rest.

MYSTERY NUMBER FOUR: WILL *PIONEER GIRL* EVER BE PUBLISHED?

All but Mrs. Wilder's most informed fans would be surprised to learn that she completed a one-volume novel of her life that has never been published. The edited manuscript has lain unpublished for sixty years, and those who have visited the Mansfield home in recent years may have noticed several references to the "about-to-be published" *Pioneer Girl*. I remember that the notices were four and five years old when I visited the home several years ago now. But no book on this material ever came to be published.

A book called *Pioneer Girl* was published, but it did not contain the one-volume novel of her life.

Even if this novel were published someday, it would not be considered top quality writing, for it was rejected by several publishers when first offered in the early 1930s. If the one-volume manuscript ever were published, it would still attract considerable attention because of its autobiographical nature. Indeed, the fact is, this book is reported to be the working outline for the entire series. The other thing that seems to keep it from being published is that it is very straightforward and factual.

Mrs. Wilder's fans realize that there are liberties in the stories. Apparently, the old *Pioneer Girl* manuscript would go a long way toward telling us how much and where.

MYSTERY NUMBER FIVE: HOW DID LAURA AND ROSE RELATE TO EACH OTHER?

This relationship has been touched upon earlier, but perhaps needs a further word here to balance the rather bleak picture presented by Dr. William Holtz in his biography of Rose titled *Ghost in the Little House*. Dr. Holtz unarguably shows that Rose's diaries reveal a daughter who both loved and at times almost loathed her mother. The question is, What to make of it? Is there a side to Mrs. Wilder and the image we have of her from the series that needs to be concealed for the sake of her reputation?

No. Most of the really troubling years between mother and daughter seem to have taken place during the 1930s when they were working together. Laura was using significant amounts of Rose's expertise to get her children's books under way. At the same time, Rose was using much of her mother's life story to craft the book *Let the Hurricane*

Roar, which would keep the family farm afloat financially. (Rose had lost her money and her parents' money in the stock market crash.)

On the other hand, Laura's extreme difficulty in organizing her own material made great demands on Rose's time so that she felt increasingly frustrated about being used at her mother's beck and call. Does any of this sound fairly normal, as opposed to psychotic, as *Ghost in the Little House* implies? Many relationships would be damaged by such a volatile mix of dependence and independence.

> Mother and daughter were happiest when they communicated— at a distance.

Mother and daughter were happiest when they communicated—at a distance—and things definitely improved between Laura and Rose as soon as Rose moved away and the Wilders could quickly return to their own house (from which they had been displaced by Rose, who had taken it over as her house and work space).

It is a testimony to the strength of family ties that mother and daughter came through their six or seven years of close proximity, collaborating and competing over the same material, with their relationship still intact.

Rather than assume the worst from Rose's diaries, we have to understand that throughout much of the terrible 1930s she suffered periodic bouts of severe depression.

These episodes drained her, darkened her vision of everything and everybody, and left her incapable of work for days on end.

Rose pulled through this dark period to find something like peace and security in her latter days. As her fortunes and those of her mother's improved, so did their relationship.

Laura and Rose by a stream on the farm

MYSTERY NUMBER SIX: DID THE BOOKS MAKE LAURA RICH?

Call it silly that we should want to know such things, but we do naturally wonder if Mrs. Wilder ended her days well off. And if well off, how well off?

We do have a few clues.

When Mrs. Wilder died, the Mansfield newspaper

speculated that Mrs. Wilder was receiving something like $18,000 a year. If that is an accurate estimate, then that number multiplied by five to allow for inflation would bring her yearly earnings to something like $90,000 by today's standards.

This figure is all the more remarkable if her publishers held her to her 1930s contracts, which specified that both *Farmer Boy* and *Little House on the Prairie* earn only a straight 5 percent of retail, rather than the 10 percent they gave her for *Little House in the Big Woods*.

Yet Laura could have gone back after the Depression was over and requested a better deal. Her agent, George Bye, could have pointed out, justly, that business conditions had improved and that Laura deserved a higher rate on *Farmer Boy* and *Little House on the Prairie*.

All of Laura's books continued to sell fantastically well throughout this period with very little promotional help from her publisher. In fact, the books sold so well in original hardcover that it was not until the middle 1950s that the publisher decided to issue a paperback edition, with the famous Garth Williams illustrations. Williams's illustrations took ten years to complete and were so hugely successful, they nearly eclipsed great work he had done on earlier children's books. Indeed, his illustrations are the only illustrations most people associate with the books.

Certainly, by the time Mrs. Wilder died, by Ozark standards she was a wealthy lady. For tax purposes her estate was valued at some $80,000, or over $400,000 by today's standards. She had some $10,000 in a bank account, an amount that would be high even by today's inflated standards.

Yet it must be admitted that this increasingly well-off lady probably never saw herself as being delivered from the economic wilderness of her early and even mature years. The Wilders never really had money of their own to spare until the early 1940s, when the accumulation of their royalties became significant. "The Man of the Place" lived his entire adult life trying to wrest a living from the land: first in cruelly dry South Dakota, then in cruelly rocky Missouri hill country.

By then, the habits of lifelong penury lay on them both. After Mr. Wilder died, Laura closed off several rooms of the house. She lived mostly in the kitchen, the dining room, and her bedroom. The outside of the old farm home that had once been a showplace of the Ozarks took on a neglected look—drain spouts askew, paint peeling.

Laura, who relished the years of her early travels, spent the last years of life close to home, contenting herself now and then with a chauffeured drive through her Ozark hills.

ABOUT THE AUTHOR

Laura Ingalls Wilder (1867–1957) began writing, at age sixty-five, a series of eight children's books about her life in the pioneer West. These books were later turned into a world-renowned TV series. We all came to know and love Laura and her family either through the TV series or through the books. Yet twenty years before she even started the series, Wilder wrote articles for regional newspapers and magazines. *Writings to Young Women* is a collection of these articles.

ABOUT THE EDITOR

Stephen W. Hines has loved Laura Ingalls Wilder's books since he was a boy, and this love is evident in the careful research and arrangement of these delightful articles. Hines graduated from the University of Kansas and received his MA in journalism from Ball State University in Muncie, Indiana. He has worked in publishing since 1979. More than six hundred thousand of his books are currently in print.